Henry Kendall

Leaves from Australian Forests

Henry Kendall

Leaves from Australian Forests

ISBN/EAN: 9783337311674

Printed in Europe, USA, Canada, Australia, Japan

Cover: Foto ©Andreas Hilbeck / pixelio.de

More available books at **www.hansebooks.com**

LEAVES FROM

AUSTRALIAN FORESTS.

BY

HENRY KENDALL.

MELBOURNE:
GEORGE ROBERTSON, 69 ELIZABETH STREET.
MDCCCLXIX.

DEDICATION.

To her, who, cast with me in trying days,
Stood in the place of health, and power, and praise;—
Who, when I thought all light was out, became
A lamp of hope that put my fears to shame;—
Who faced for love's sole sake the life austere
That waits upon the man of letters here;—
Who, unawares, her deep affection showed,
By many a touching little wifely mode;—
Whose spirit self-denying, dear, divine,
Its sorrows hid, so it might lessen mine,—
To her, my bright best friend, I dedicate
This book of songs. 'Twill help to compensate
For much neglect. The act, if not the rhyme,
Will touch her heart and lead her to the time
Of trials past. That which is most intense
Within these leaves is of her influence;
And if aught here is sweetened with a tone
Sincere, like love, it came of love alone.

CONTENTS.

	PAGE
PREFATORY SONNETS	1
THE HUT BY THE BLACK SWAMP	3
SEPTEMBER IN AUSTRALIA	7
GHOST GLEN	10
DAPHNE	13
THE WARRIGAL	16
EUROCLYDON	19
ARALUEN	24
AT EUROMA	28
ILLA CREEK	30
MOSS ON A WALL	33
CAMPASPE	36
ON A CATTLE TRACK	39
TO DAMASCUS	42
BELL BIRDS	45
A DEATH IN THE BUSH	48
A SPANISH LOVE SONG	58
THE LAST OF HIS TRIBE	60
ARAKOON	62
THE VOYAGE OF TELEGONUS	65

SITTING BY THE FIRE	74
CLEONE	76
CHARLES HARPUR	78
GOD HELP OUR MEN AT SEA	81
COOGEE	83
OGYGES	87
BY THE SEA	92
SONG OF THE CATTLE HUNTERS	93
KING SAUL AT GILBOA	95
IN THE VALLEY	101
TWELVE SONNETS	103
SUTHERLAND'S GRAVE	115
SYRINX	118
ON THE PAROO	121
FAITH IN GOD	125
MOUNTAIN MOSS	127
THE GLEN OF ARRAWATTA	130
EUTERPE	139
ELLEN RAY	143
AT DUSK	145
SAFI	148
DANIEL HENRY DENIEHY	153
MEROPE	156
AFTER THE HUNT	160
ROSE LORRAINE	161

I.

I PURPOSED once to take my pen and write
    Not songs like some tormented and awry
    With Passion, but a cunning harmony
Of words and music caught from glen and height,
And lucid colours born of woodland light,
    And shining places where the sea-streams lie;
But this was when the heat of youth glowed white,
    And, since, I've put the faded purpose by.
I have no faultless fruits to offer you
    Who read this book; but certain syllables
    Herein are borrowed from unfooted dells,
And secret hollows dear to noontide dew;
And these at least, though far between and few,
    May catch the sense like subtle forest spells.

II.

So take these kindly, even though there be
   Some notes that unto other lyres belong :
   Stray echoes from the elder sons of Song ;
And think how from its neighbouring, native sea
The pensive shell doth borrow melody.
   I would not do the lordly masters wrong,
   By filching fair words from the shining throng
Whose music haunts me, as the wind a tree!
   Lo, when a stranger, in soft Syrian glooms
Shot through with sunset, treads the cedar dells,
And hears the breezy ring of elfin bells
     Far down by where the white-haired cataract booms,
He, faint with sweetness caught from forest smells,
   Bears thence, unwitting, plunder of perfumes.

LEAVES FROM AUSTRALIAN FORESTS.

THE HUT BY THE BLACK SWAMP.

Now comes the fierce North-Easter, bound
　About with cloud and racks of rain;
And dry dead leaves go whirling round
　In rings of dust, and sigh like Pain
　　Across the plain.

Now Twilight, with a shadowy hand
　Of wild dominionship, doth keep
Strong hold of hollow straits of land;
　And watery sounds are loud and deep
　　By gap and steep.

THE HUT BY THE BLACK SWAMP.

Keen fitful gusts that fly before
    The wings of Storm when Day hath shut
Its eyes on mountains, flaw by flaw,
    Fleet down by whistling boxtree-but
        Against the Hut.

And ringed and girt with lurid pomp
    Far eastern cliffs start up and take
Thick steaming vapours from a swamp
    That lieth like a great blind lake
        Of face opaque.

The moss that like a tender grief
    About an English ruin clings—
What time the wan autumnal leaf
    Faints after many wanderings
        On windy wings—

That gracious growth whose quiet green
    Is as a love in days austere,
Was never seen—hath never been
    On slab or roof, deserted here
        For many a year.

Nor comes the bird whose speech is song—
    Whose songs are silvery syllables
That unto glimmering woods belong,
    And deep meandering mountain-dells
        By yellow wells.

But rather here the wild dog halts,
   And lifts the paw, and looks, and howls;
And here, in ruined forest-vaults,
   Abide dim, dark, death-featured owls,
     Like monks in cowls.

Across this Hut the nettle runs;
   And livid adders make their lair
In corners dank from lack of suns;
   And out of fetid furrows stare
     The growths that scare.

Here Summer's grasp of fire is laid
   On bark and slabs that rot and breed
Squat ugly things of deadly shade—
   The scorpion, and the spiteful seed
     Of centipede.

Unhallowed thunders harsh and dry,
   And flaming noontides mute with heat,
Beneath the breathless, brazen sky,
   Upon these rifted rafters beat
     With torrid feet.

And night by night, the fitful gale
   Doth carry past the bittern's boom,
The dingo's yell, the plover's wail,
   While lumbering shadows start, and loom,
     And hiss through gloom.

THE HUT BY THE BLACK SWAMP.

No sign of grace—no hope of green,
   Cool-blossomed seasons marks the spot;
But, chained to iron doom, I ween,
   'Tis left, like skeleton, to rot
     Where ruth is not.

For on this Hut hath Murder writ
   With bloody fingers hellish things;
And God will never visit it
   With flower or leaf of sweet-faced Springs,
     Or gentle wings.

SEPTEMBER IN AUSTRALIA.

Grey Winter hath gone, like a wearisome guest,
    And, behold, for repayment,
September comes in with the wind of the West,
    And the Spring in her raiment!
The ways of the frost have been filled of the flowers
    While the forest discovers
Wild wings with the halo of hyaline hours,
    And a music of lovers.

September, the maid with the swift, silver feet!
    She glides, and she graces
The valleys of coolness, the slopes of the heat,
    With her blossomy traces.
Sweet month with a mouth that is made of a rose,
    She lightens and lingers
In spots where the harp of the evening glows,
    Attuned by her fingers.

The stream from its home in the hollow hill slips
    In a darling old fashion;
And the day goeth down with a song on its lips,
    Whose key-note is passion.
Far out in the fierce bitter front of the sea,
    I stand and remember
Dead things that were brothers and sisters of thee,
    Resplendent September.

The West, when it blows at the fall of the noon,
    And beats on the beaches,
Is filled with a tender and tremulous tune
    That touches and teaches:
The stories of Youth, of the burden of Time,
    And the death of Devotion,
Come back with the wind, and are themes of the rhyme,
    In the waves of the ocean.

We, having a secret to others unknown,
    In the cool mountain-mosses,
May whisper together, September, alone
    Of our loves and our losses.
One word for her beauty, and one for the grace
    She gave to the hours;
And then we may kiss her, and suffer her face
    To sleep with the flowers.

SEPTEMBER IN AUSTRALIA.

High places that knew of the gold and the white
   On the forehead of Morning,
Now darken and quake, and the steps of the Night
   Are heavy with warning!
Her voice in the distance is lofty and loud,
   Through the echoing gorges;
She hath hidden her eyes in a mantle of cloud,
   And her feet in the surges!

On the tops of the hills; on the turreted cones—
   Chief temples of thunder—
The gale, like a ghost, in the middle watch moans,
   Gliding over and under.
The sea, flying white through the rack and the rain,
   Leapeth wild at the forelands;
And the plover, whose cry is like passion with pain,
   Complains in the moorlands.

O, season of changes—of shadow and shine—
   September the splendid!
My song hath no music to mingle with thine,
   And its burden is ended:
But thou, being born of the winds and the sun,
   By mountain, by river,
May lighten and listen, and loiter and run,
   With thy voices for ever.

GHOST GLEN.

"Shut your ears, stranger, or, turn from Ghost Glen
    now,
For the paths are grown over; untrodden by men
    now—
Shut your ears, stranger!" saith the grey mother,
    crooning
Her sorcery Runic, when sets the half moon in!

To-night the North-Easter goes travelling slowly,
But it never stoops down to that Hollow unholy—
To-night it rolls loud on the ridges red-litten,
But it *cannot* abide in that Forest sin-smitten!

For over the pitfall the moondew is thawing,
And, with never a body, two shadows stand sawing!
The wraiths of two sawyers *(step under and under)*,
Who did a foul murder, and were blackened with
    thunder!

Whenever the storm-wind comes driven and driving,
Through the blood-spattered timber you may see the
    saw striving—
You may see the saw heaving, and falling, and heaving,
Whenever the sea-creek is chafing and grieving!

And across a burnt body, as black as an adder,
Sits the sprite of a sheep-dog!—was ever sight sadder!
For as the dry thunder splits louder and faster,
This sprite of a sheep-dog howls for his master!

"Oh! count your beads deftly," saith the grey mother,
    crooning
Her sorcery Runic, when sets the half moon in!
And well may she mutter, for the dark hollow laughter
You will hear in the sawpits, and the bloody logs after!

Ay, count your beads deftly, and keep your ways wary,
For the sake of the Saviour and sweet Mother Mary!
Pray for your peace in these perilous places,
And pray for the laying of horrible faces!

One starts with a forehead wrinkled and livid,
Aghast at the lightnings sudden and vivid!
One telleth with curses the gold that they drew
    there
(Ah! cross your breast humbly) from him whom
    they slew there!

The stranger who came from the loved—the
    romantic
Island that sleeps on the moaning Atlantic;
Leaving behind him a patient home yearning
For the steps in the distance, never returning;—

Who was left in the Forest, shrunken, and starkly
Burnt by his slayers (so men have said darkly):
With the half-crazy sheep-dog, who cowered beside
    there
And yelled at the silence, and marvelled, and died
    there!

Yea, cross your breast humbly, and hold your breath
    tightly,
Or fly for your life from those shadows unsightly;
From the set staring features (cold, and so young
    too!)
And the death on the lips that a mother hath clung to.

I tell you, the Bushman is braver than most men,
Who even in daylight doth go through the Ghost Glen!
Although in that Hollow, unholy and lonely,
He sees the dank sawpits and bloody logs only!

DAPHNE.

Daphne! Ladon's daughter, Daphne! Set thyself in silver light,
Take thy thoughts of fairest texture, weave them into words of white—
Weave the rhyme of rose-lipped Daphne, nymph of wooded stream and shade,
Flying love of bright Apollo,—fleeting type of faultless maid!
She, when followed from the forelands by the lord of lyre and lute,
Sped towards far-singing waters, past deep gardens flushed with fruit;
Took the path against Peneus, panted by its yellow banks;
Turned, and looked, and flew the faster through grey-tufted thicket ranks;
Flashed amongst high flowered sedges: leaped across the brook, and ran
Down to where the fourfold shadows of a nether glade began;

There she dropped, like falling Hesper, heavy hair of
    radiant head
Hiding all the young abundance of her beauty's
    white and red.

Came the yellow-tressed Far-darter—came the god
    whose feet are fire,
On his lips the name of Daphne, in his eyes a great
    desire;
Fond, full lips of lord and lover, sad because of suit
    denied;
Clear, grey eyes made keen by passion, panting,
    pained, unsatisfied.
Here he turned, and there he halted, now he paused,
    and now he flew,
Swifter than his sister's arrows, through soft dells of
    dreamy dew.
Vext with gleams of Ladon's daughter, dashed along
    the son of Jove,
Fast upon flower-trammelled Daphne fleeting on from
    grove to grove;
Flights of seawind hard behind him, breaths of bleak
    and whistling straits;
Drifts of driving cloud above him, like a troop of
    fierce-eyed fates!
So he reached the water-shallows; then he stayed his
    steps, and heard

Daphne drop upon the grasses, fluttering like a
    wounded bird.

Was there help for Ladon's daughter? Saturn's son
    is high and just:
Did he come between her beauty and the fierce Far-
    darter's lust?
As she lay, the helpless maiden, caught and bound in
    fast eclipse,
Did the lips of god drain pleasure from her sweet and
    swooning lips?
Now that these and all Love's treasures blushed,
    before the spoiler, bare,
Was the wrong that shall be nameless done, and seen,
    and suffered there?
No! for Zeus is King and Father. Weary nymph
    and fiery god,
Bend the knee alike before him—he is kind, and he
    is lord!
Therefore sing how clear-browed Pallas—Pallas, friend
    of prayerful maid,
Lifted dazzling Daphne lightly, bore her down the
    breathless glade,
Did the thing that Zeus commanded: so it came to
    pass that he
Who had chased a white-armed virgin, caught at her,
    and clasped a tree.

THE WARRIGAL.*

Through forest boles the stormwind rolls,
    Vext of the sea-driven rain,
And up in the clift, through many a rift,
    The voices of torrents complain.
The sad marsh-fowl and the lonely owl
    Are heard in the fog-wreaths grey,
When the Warrigal wakes, and listens, and takes
    To the woods that shelter the prey.

In the gully-deeps, the blind creek sleeps;
    And the silver, showery, moon
Glides over the hills, and floats, and fills,
    And dreams in the dark lagoon;
While halting hard by the station yard,
    Aghast at the hut-flame nigh,
The Warrigal yells, and the flats and fells
    Are loud with his dismal cry.

* The Wild Dog.

THE WARRIGAL.

On the topmost peak of mountains bleak,
   The south wind sobs, and strays
Through moaning pine, and turpentine,
   And the rippling runnel ways;
And strong streams flow, and great mists go,
   Where the Warrigal starts to hear
The watch-dog's bark break sharp in the dark,
   And flees like a phantom of Fear!

The swift rains beat, and the thunders fleet
   On the wings of the fiery gale,
And down in the glen of pool and fen,
   The wild gums whistle and wail,
As over the plains, and past the chains
   Of waterholes glimmering deep,
The Warrigal flies from the Shepherd's cries,
   And the clamour of dogs and sheep.

The Warrigal's lair is pent in bare
   Black rocks at the gorge's mouth:
It is set in ways where Summer strays
   With the sprites of flame and drouth;
But when the heights are touched with lights
   Of hoarfrost, sleet, and shine,
His bed is made of the dead grass-blade
   And the leaves of the windy pine.

He roves through the lands of sultry sands,
    He hunts in the iron range,
Untamed as surge of the far sea verge,
    And fierce and fickle and strange.
The white man's track and the haunts of the black
    He shuns, and shudders to see ;
For his joy he tastes in lonely wastes
    Where his mates are torrent and tree.

EUROCLYDON.

On the storm-cloven Cape
    The bitter waves roll
    With the bergs of the Pole,
And the darks and the damps of the Northern Sea:
    For the storm-cloven Cape
    Is an alien Shape
With a fearful face; and it moans, and it stands
    Outside all lands
      Everlastingly!

When the fruits of the year
    Have been gathered in Spain;
    And the Indian rain
Is rich on the evergreen lands of the Sun;

EUROCLYDON.

There comes to this Cape—
To this alien Shape,
As the waters beat in and the echoes troop forth,
The Wind of the North,
Euroclydon! ✦

And the wilted thyme,
And the patches past
Of the nettles cast
In the drift of the rift, and the broken rime,
Are tumbled and blown
To every zone
With the famished glede, and the plovers thinned
By this fourfold Wind—
This Wind sublime!

On the wrinkled hills
By starts and fits
The wild Moon sits;
And the rindles fill, and flash, and fall
In the way of her light,
Through the straitened night,
When the sea-heralds clamour, and elves of the war
In the torrents afar,
Hold festival!

✦ A impetuous S.E. wind raising fatal waves in Mediterranean Sea!

From ridge to ridge
    The polar fires
    On the naked spires
With a foreign splendour, flit and flow ;
    And clough and cave
    And architrave,
Have a blood-coloured glamour on roof and on wall,
    Like a nether hall
    In the hells below!

The dead dry lips
    Of the ledges, split
    By the thunder fit
And the stress of the sprites of the forkéd flame,
    Anon break out
    With a shriek and a shout,
Like a hard bitter laughter cracked and thin
    From a ghost with a sin
    Too dark for a name!

And, all thro' the year,
    The fierce seas run
    From sun to sun,
Across the face of a vacant world!

And the Wind flies forth
From the wild white North,
That shivers and harries the heart of things,
And shapes with its wings
A Chaos uphurled!

Like one who sees
A rebel light
In the thick of the night,
As he stumbles and staggers on summits afar—
Who looks to it still,
Up hill and hill,
With a steadfast hope (though the ways be deep,
And rough, and steep),
Like a steadfast star;

So I, that stand
On the outermost peaks
Of peril, with cheeks
Blue with the salts of a frosty Sea,
Have learnt to wait
With an eye elate
And a heart intent, for the fuller blaze
Of the Beauty that rays
Like a glimpse for me—

Of the Beauty that grows
Whenever I hear
The Winds of Fear
From the tops and the bases of barrenness call:
And the duplicate lore
Which I learn evermore,
Is of Harmony filling and rounding the Storm,
And the marvellous Form
That governs all!

ARALUEN.

River, myrtle-rimmed, and set
    Deep amongst unfooted dells—
Daughter of grey hills of wet,
    Born by mossed and yellow wells—

Now that soft September lays
    Tender hands on thee and thine,
Let me think of blue-eyed days,
    Star-like flowers, and leaves of shine !

Cities soil the life with rust:
    Water-banks are cool and sweet:
River, tired of noise and dust
    Here I come to rest my feet.

ARALUEN.

Now the month from shade to sun
    Fleets and sings supremest songs,
Now the wilful woodwinds run
    Through the tangled cedar throngs.

Here are cushioned tufts and turns
    Where the sumptuous noontide lies.
Here are seen by flags and ferns
    Summer's large luxurious eyes.

On this spot wan Winter casts
    Eyes of ruth, and spares its green
From his bitter sea-nursed blasts,
    Spears of rain and hailstones keen.

Rather here abideth Spring,
    Lady of a lovely land,
Dear to leaf and fluttering wing,
    Deep in blooms—by breezes fanned.

Faithful friend beyond the main—
    Friend that Time nor Change makes cold—
Now, like ghosts, return again
    Pallid perished days of old.

ARALUEN.

Ah, the days—the old, old theme
    Never stale, but never new,
Floating, like a pleasant dream,
    Back to me and back to you.

Since we rested on these slopes,
    Seasons fierce have beaten down
Ardent loves and blossoming hopes—
    Loves that lift, and hopes that crown.

But, believe me, still mine eyes
    Often fill with light that springs
From <u>divinity, which lies</u>
    <u>Ever at the heart of things.</u>

Solace do I sometimes find
    Where you used to hear with me
Songs of stream and forest-wind,
    Tones of wave and harp-like tree.

Araluen! home of dreams!
    Fairer for its flowerful glade
Than the face of Persian streams,
    Or the slopes of Syrian shade.

Why should I still love it so?
   Friend and brother far away,
Ask the winds that come and go,
   What hath brought me here to-day.

Evermore of you I think,
   When the leaves begin to fall,
Where our river breaks its brink,
   And a rest is over all.

Evermore in quiet lands,
   Friend of mine beyond the sea,
Memory comes with cunning hands,
   Stays, and paints your face for me.

AT EUROMA.

They built his mound of the rough red ground,
    By the dip of a desert dell,
Where all things sweet are killed by the heat,
    And scattered o'er flat and fell.
In a burning zone they left him alone,
    Past the uttermost western plain;
And the nightfall dim heard his funeral hymn
    In the voices of wind and rain.

The songs austere of the forests drear,
    And the echoes of clift and cave,
When the dark is keen where the storm hath been,
    Fleet over the far-away grave.
And through the days when the torrid rays
    Strike down on a coppery gloom,
Some spirit grieves in the perished leaves
    Whose theme is that desolate tomb.

No human foot, or paw of brute,
   Halts now where the stranger sleeps;
But cloud and star his fellows are,
   And the rain that sobs and weeps.
The dingo yells by the far iron fells,
   The plover is loud in the range,
But they never come near to the slumberer here,
   Whose rest is a rest without change.

Ah! in his life, had he mother or wife,
   To wait for his step on the floor?
Did Beauty wax dim while watching for him
   Who passed through the threshold no more?
Doth it trouble his head?　He is one with the dead;
   He lies by the alien streams;
And sweeter than sleep is death that is deep
   And unvexed by the lordship of dreams.

ILLA CREEK.

A strong sea-wind flies up and sings
   Across the blown-wet border,
Whose stormy echo runs and rings
   Like bells in wild disorder.

Fierce breath hath vext the foreland's face,
   It glistens, glooms, and glistens;
But deep within this quiet place
   Sweet Illa lies and listens.

Sweet Illa of the shining sands,
   She sleeps in shady hollows
Where August flits with flowerful hands
   And silver Summer follows.

ILLA CREEK.

Far up the naked hills is heard
    A noise of many waters;
But green-haired Illa lies unstirred
    Amongst her star-like daughters.

The tempest pent in moaning ways
    Awakes the shepherd yonder;
But Illa dreams, unknown to days
    Whose wings are wind and thunder.

Here fairy hands and floral feet
    Are brought by bright October;
Here stained with grapes, and smit with heat,
    Comes Autumn sweet and sober.

Here lovers rest, what time the red
    And yellow colours mingle,
And Daylight droops with dying head
    Beyond the western dingle.

And here, from month to month, the time
    Is kissed by Peace and Pleasure,
While Nature sings her woodland rhyme
    And hoards her woodland treasure.

ILLA CREEK.

Ah, Illa Creek! ere Evening spreads
    Her wings o'er towns unshaded,
How oft we seek thy mossy beds
    To lave our foreheads faded!

For, let me whisper, then we find
    The strength that lives, nor falters,
In wood and water, waste and wind,
    And hidden mountain altars.

MOSS ON A WALL.

Dim dreams it hath of singing ways,
   Of far-off woodland water-heads,
And shining ends of April days
   Amongst the yellow runnel beds.

Stoop closer to the ruined wall,
   Wherein the wilful wilding sleeps,
As if its home were waterfall
   By dripping clefts and shadowy steeps!

A little waif, whose beauty takes
   A touching tone, because it dwells
So far away from mountain lakes,
   And lily leaves, and lightening fells.

Deep hidden in delicious floss
   It nestles, sister, from the heat:
A gracious growth of tender moss,
   Whose nights are soft, whose days are sweet.

Swift gleams across its petals run,
   With winds that hum a pleasant tune:
Serene surprises of the sun,
   And whispers from the lips of Noon.

The evening-coloured apple-trees
   Are faint with July's frosty breath;
But lo, this stranger getteth ease
   And shines amidst the strays of Death!

And at the turning of the year,
   When August wanders in the cold,
The raiment of the nursling here
   Is rich with green and glad with gold.

O, friend of mine, to one whose eyes
   Are vext because of alien things,
For ever in the wall moss lies
   The peace of hills and hidden springs.

MOSS ON A WALL.

From faithless lips and fickle lights
   The tired pilgrim sets his face,
And thinketh here of sounds and sights
   In many a lovely forest-place.

And when by sudden fits and starts
   The sunset on the moss doth burn,
He often dreams, and lo, the marts
   And streets are changed to dells of fern!

For, let me say, the wilding placed
   By hands unseen amongst these stones,
Restores a Past by Time effaced,
   Lost loves and long-forgotten tones!

As sometimes songs and scenes of old
   Come faintly unto you and me,
When winds are wailing in the cold,
   And rains are sobbing on the sea.

CAMPASPE.

Turn from the ways of this Woman! Campaspe we
    call her by name—
She is fairer than flowers of the fire—she is brighter
    than brightness of flame.
As a song that strikes swift to the heart with the
    beat of the blood of the South,
And a light and a leap and a smart, is the play of her
    perilous mouth.
Her eyes are as splendours that break in the rain at
    the set of the sun,
But turn from the steps of Campaspe—a Woman to
    look at and shun!

Dost thou know of the cunning of Beauty? take
    heed to thyself and beware
Of the trap in the droop in the raiment—the snare
    in the folds of the hair!

She is fulgent in flashes of pearl, the breeze with her
    breathing is sweet,
But fly from the face of the girl—there is death in
    the fall of her feet!
Is she maiden or marvel of marble? O rather a
    tigress at wait
To pounce on thy soul for her pastime—a leopard for
    love or for hate.

Woman of shadow and furnace! she biteth her lips
    to restrain
Speech that springs out when she sleepeth, by the
    stirs and the starts of her pain.
As music half-shapen of sorrow, with its wants and
    its infinite wail,
Is the voice of Campaspe, the beauty at bay with her
    passion dead-pale.
Go out from the courts of her loving, nor tempt the
    fierce dance of desire
Where thy life would be shrivelled like stubble in
    the stress and the fervour of fire!

<u>I know of one, gentle as moonlight—she is sad as
    the shine of the moon,
But touching the ways of her eyes are: she comes
    to my soul like a tune—</u>

Like a tune that is filled with faint voices of the
    loved and the lost and the lone,
Doth this stranger abide with my silence: like a
    tune with a tremulous tone.
The leopard, we call her, Campaspe! I pluck at a
    rose and I stir
To think of this sweet-hearted maiden—what name
    is too tender for her?

ON A CATTLE TRACK.

Where the strength of dry thunder splits hill-rocks
    asunder,
  And the shouts of the desert-wind break,
By the gullies of deepness, and ridges of steepness,
  Lo, the cattle-track twists like a snake!
Like a sea of dead embers burnt white by Decembers,
  A plain to the left of it lies;
And six fleeting horses dash down the creek-courses,
  With the terror of thirst in their eyes.

The false strength of fever, that deadly deceiver,
  Gives foot to each famishing beast;
And over lands rotten, by rain-winds forgotten,
  The mirage gleams out in the east.
Ah! the waters are hidden, from riders and ridden,
  In a stream where the cattle-track dips;
And Death on their faces is scoring fierce traces,
  And the drouth is a fire on their lips.

It is far to the Station, and gaunt Desolation
   Is a spectre that glooms in the way;
Like a *red* smoke the air is, like a hell-light its glare is,
   And as flame are the feet of the day.
The wastes are like metal that forges unsettle
   When the heat of the furnace is white;
And the cool breeze that bloweth when an English
      sun goeth,
   Is unknown to the wild Desert Night.

A cry of distress there! a horseman the less there!
   The mock-waters shine like a moon!
It is "speed, and speed faster from this hole of
      disaster,
   "And hurrah for yon God-sent lagoon."
Doth a devil deceive them? Ah, now let us leave
      them,
   We are burdened in life with the sad;
Our portion is trouble, our joy is a bubble;
   And the gladdest is never too glad.

From the pale tracts of peril, past mountain heads
      sterile,
   To a sweet river shadowed with reeds
Where Summer steps lightly, and Winter beams
      brightly,
   The hoof-rutted cattle-track leads.

There soft is the moonlight, and tender the noonlight;
    There fiery things falter and fall ;
And there, may be seen, now, the gold and the green, now,
    And the wings of a peace over all.

Hush, bittern and plover ! Go, wind, to thy cover
    Away by the snow-smitten Pole !
The rotten leaf falleth, the forest rain calleth ;
    And what is the end of the whole ?
Some men are successful after seasons distressful,
    [Now, masters, the drift of my tale]
But the brink of salvation is a lair of damnation
    For others who struggle, yet fail.

TO DAMASCUS.

WHERE the sinister sun of the Syrians beat
   On the brittle bright stubble,
And the camels fell back from the swords of the heat,
Came Saul with a fire in the soles of his feet,
   And a forehead of trouble.

And terrified faces to left and to right,
   Before and behind him,
Fled away with the speed of a maddening fright,
To the cloughs of the bat, and the chasms of night,
Each hoping the zealot would fail in his flight
   To find him and bind him.

For, behold you, the strong man of Tarsus came
    down
  With breathings of slaughter,
From the priests of the city, the chiefs of the town,
(The lords with the sword, and the sires with the
    gown),
To harry the Christians, and trample, and drown,
  And waste them like water.

He was *ever* a fighter, this son of the Jews—
  A fighter in earnest;
And the Lord took delight in the strength of his
    thews,
For He knew he was one of the few He could choose
To fight out His battles, and carry His news
Of a marvellous Truth through the dark, and the
    dews,
  And the desert-lands furnaced!

He knew he was one of the few He could take
  For His Mission supernal;
Whose feet would not falter, whose limbs would not
    ache,
Through the waterless lands of the thorn and the
    snake,
And the ways of the wild—bearing up for the sake
  Of a Beauty eternal.

And therefore the road to Damascus was burned
    With a swift, sudden brightness;
While Saul, with his face in the bitter dust, learned
Of the sin which he did, ere he tumbled, and turned
    Aghast at God's whiteness!

Of the sin which he did, ere he covered his head
    From the strange revelation.
But, thereafter, you know of the life that he led;
How he preached to the peoples, and suffered, and sped
With the wonderful words which his Master had said,
    From nation to nation.

Now would we be like him, who suffer and see,
    If the Chooser should choose us!
For I tell you, brave brothers, whoever you be,
It is right, till all learn to look further, and see,
    That our Master should use us!

It is right, till all learn to discover and class,
    That our Master should task us:
For now we may judge of the Truth through a glass;
And the road over which they must evermore pass,
Who would think for the many, and fight for the
    mass,
    Is the road to Damascus.

BELL BIRDS.

By channels of coolness the echoes are calling,
And down the dim gorges I hear the creek falling :
It lives in the mountain where moss and the sedges
Touch with their beauty the banks and the ledges.
Through breaks of the cedar and sycamore bowers
Struggles the light that is love to the flowers ;
And, softer than slumber, and sweeter than singing,
The notes of the bell-birds are running and ringing.

The silver-voiced bell-birds, the darlings of daytime!
They sing in September their songs of the May-time;
When shadows wax strong, and the thunder-bolts hurtle,
They hide with their fear in the leaves of the myrtle;

When rain and the sunbeams shine mingled together,
They start up like fairies that follow fair weather;
And straightway the hues of their feathers unfolden
Are the green and the purple, the blue and the golden.

October, the maiden of bright yellow tresses,
Loiters for love in these cool wildernesses;
Loiters, knee-deep, in the grasses, to listen,
Where dripping rocks gleam and the leafy pools glisten:
Then is the time when the water-moons splendid
Break with their gold, and are scattered or blended
Over the creeks, till the woodlands have warning
Of songs of the bell-bird and wings of the Morning.

Welcome as waters unkissed by the summers
Are the voices of bell-birds to thirsty far-comers.
When fiery December sets foot in the forest,
And the need of the wayfarer presses the sorest,
Pent in the ridges for ever and ever
The bell-birds direct him to spring and to river,
With ring and with ripple, like runnels whose torrents
Are toned by the pebbles and leaves in the currents.

Often I sit, looking back to a childhood,
Mixt with the sights and the sounds of the wildwood,
Longing for power and the sweetness to fashion,
Lyrics with beats like the heart-beats of Passion;—
Songs interwoven of lights and of laughters
Borrowed from bell-birds in far forest-rafters;
So I might keep in the city and alleys
The beauty and strength of the deep mountain valleys:
Charming to slumber the pain of my losses
With glimpses of creeks and a vision of mosses.

A DEATH IN THE BUSH.

The hut was built of bark and shrunken slabs
That wore the marks of many rains, and showed
Dry flaws, wherein had crept and nestled rot.
Moreover, round the bases of the bark
Were left the tracks of flying forest-fires,
As you may see them on the lower bole
Of every elder of the native woods.

For, ere the early settlers came and stocked
These wilds with sheep and kine, the grasses grew
So that they took the passing pilgrim in,
And whelmed him, like a running sea, from sight.

And therefore, through the fiercer summer months,
While all the swamps were rotten—while the flats
Were baked and broken; when the clayey rifts

Yawned wide, half-choked with drifted herbage past,
Spontaneous flames would burst from thence, and race
Across the prairies all day long.

                              At night
The winds were up, and then with fourfold speed,
A harsh gigantic growth of smoke and fire
Would roar along the bottoms, in the wake
Of fainting flocks of parrots, wallaroos,
And 'wildered wild things, scattering right and left,
For safety vague, throughout the general gloom.

Anon, the nearer hill-side growing trees
Would take the surges; thus, from bough to bough,
Was borne the flaming terror! Bole and spire,
Rank after rank, now pillared, ringed, and rolled
In blinding blaze, stood out against the dead
Down-smothered dark, for fifty leagues away.

For fifty leagues! and when the winds were strong,
For fifty more! But, in the olden time,
These fires were counted as the harbingers
Of life-essential storms; since out of smoke
And heat there came across the midnight ways
Abundant comfort, with upgathered clouds,
And runnels babbling of a plenteous fall.

So comes the Southern gale at evenfall
(The swift "brickfielder" of the local folk)
About the streets of Sydney, when the dust
Lies burnt on glaring windows, and the men
Look forth from doors of drouth, and drink the change
With thirsty haste and that most thankful cry
Of, "here it is—the cool, bright, blessed rain!"

The hut, I say, was built of bark and slabs,
And stood, the centre of a clearing, hemmed
By hurdle-yards, and ancients of the blacks:
These moped about their lazy fires, and sang
Wild ditties of the old days, with a sound
Of sorrow, like an everlasting wind,
Which mingled with the echoes of the noon,
And moaned amongst the noises of the night.

From thence a cattle-track, with link to link,
Ran off against the fishpools, to the gap,
Which sets you face to face with gleaming miles
Of broad Orara, winding in amongst
Black, barren ridges, where the nether spurs
Are fenced about by cotton-scrub, and grass
Blue-bitten with the salt of many droughts.

'Twas here the shepherd housed him every night,
And faced the prospect like a patient soul;

Borne up by some vague hope of better days,
And God's fine blessing in his faithful wife;
Until the humour of his malady
Took cunning changes from the good to bad,
And laid him lastly on a bed of death.

Two months thereafter, when the summer heat
Had roused the serpent from his rotten lair,
And made a noise of locusts in the boughs,
It came to this, that, as the blood-red sun
Of one fierce day of many slanted down
Obliquely past the nether jags of peaks
And gulfs of mist, the tardy night came vexed
By belted clouds, and scuds that wheeled and whirled
To left and right about the brazen clifts
Of ridges, rigid with a leaden gloom.

Then took the cattle to the forest camps
With vacant terror, and the hustled sheep
Stood dumb against the hurdles, even like
A fallen patch of shadowed mountain snow;
And ever through the curlew's call afar
The storm grew on, while round the stinted slabs
Sharp snaps and hisses came, and went, and came,
The huddled tokens of a mighty blast
Which ran with an exceeding bitter cry
Across the tumbled fragments of the hills,
And through the sluices of the gorge and glen.

So, therefore, all about the shepherd's hut
That space was mute, save when the fastened dog,
Without a kennel, caught a passing glimpse
Of firelight moving through the lighted chinks;
For then he knew the hints of warmth within,
And stood, and set his great pathetic eyes,
In wind and wet, imploring to be loosed.

Not often now the watcher left the couch
Of him she watched; since, in his fitful sleep,
His lips would stir to wayward themes, and close
With bodeful catches. Once she moved away,
Half-deafened by terrific claps, and stooped,
And looked without; to see a pillar dim
Of gathered gusts and fiery rain.

        Anon,
The sick man woke, and, startled by the noise,
Stared round the room, with dull delirious sight,
At this wild thing and that; for, through his eyes,
The place took fearful shapes, and fever showed
Strange crosswise lights about his pillow-head.
He, catching there at some phantasmic help,
Sat upright on the bolster, with a cry
Of, "Where is Jesus?—it is bitter cold!"
And then, because the thundercalls outside
Were mixed for him with slanders of the Past,

He called his weeping wife by name, and said,
"Come closer, darling! we shall speed away
Across the seas, and seek some mountain home,
Shut in from liars, and the wicked words
That track us day and night, and night and day."

So waned the sad refrain. And those poor lips,
Whose latest phrases were for peace, grew mute,
And into everlasting silence passed.

As fares a swimmer who hath lost his breath
In 'wildering seas afar from any help—
Who, fronting Death, can never realise
The dreadful Presence, but is prone to clutch
At every weed upon the weltering wave;
So fared the watcher, poring o'er the last
Of him she loved, with dazed and stupid stare;
Half conscious of the sudden loss and lack
Of all that bound her life, but yet without
The power to take her mighty sorrow in.

Then came a patch or two of starry sky;
And through a reef of cloven thunder-cloud
The soft Moon looked: a patient face beyond
The fierce impatient shadows of the slopes,
And the harsh voices of the broken hills!

A patient face, and one which came and wrought
A lovely silence like a silver mist
Across the rainy relics of the storm.

For in the breaks and pauses of her light
The gale died out in gusts; yet, evermore
About the roof-tree, on the dripping eaves,
The damp wind loitered; and a fitful drift
Sloped through the silent curtains, and athwart
The dead.

   There, when the glare had dropped behind
A mighty ridge of gloom, the woman turned
And sat in darkness face to face with God,
And said—"I know," she said, "that Thou art wise;
That when we build and hope, and hope and build,
And see our best things fall, it comes to pass
For evermore that we must turn to Thee!
And therefore now, because I cannot find
The faintest token of Divinity
In this my latest sorrow, let Thy light
Inform mine eyes, so I may learn to look
On something past the sight which shuts, and blinds,
And seems to drive me wholly, Lord, from Thee."

Now waned the moon beyond complaining depths;
And, as the dawn looked forth from showery woods
(Whereon had dropt a hint of red and gold),

There went about the crooked cavern-eaves
Low flute-like echoes with a noise of wings
And waters flying down far-hidden fells.
Then might be seen the solitary owl,
Perched in the clefts ; scared at the coming light,
And staring outward (like a sea-shelled thing
Chased to his cover by some bright fierce foe)
As at a monster in the middle waste.

At last the great kingfisher came and called
Across the hollows loud with early whips,
And lighted, laughing, on the shepherd's hut,
And roused the widow from a swoon like death.

This day, and after it was noised abroad,
By blacks, and straggling horsemen on the roads,
That he was dead " who had been sick so long,"
There flocked a troop from far-surrounding runs
To see their neighbour and to bury him.
And men who had forgotten how to cry
(Rough flinty fellows of the native bush)
Now learned the bitter way, beholding there
The wasted shadow of an iron frame
Brought down so low by years of fearful pain ;
And marking, too, the woman's gentle face,
And all the pathos in her moaned reply
Of " masters, we have lived in better days."

One stooped—a stockman from the nearer hills—
To loose his wallet-strings, from whence he took
A bag of tea, and laid it on her lap;
Then, sobbing, " God will help you, missus, yet,"
He sought his horse with most bewildered eyes,
And, spurring swiftly, galloped down the glen.

Where black Orara nightly chafes his brink,
Midway between lamenting lines of oak
And Warra's gap, the shepherd's grave was built.
And there the wild-dog pauses, in the midst
Of moonless watches: howling through the gloom
At hopeless shadows flitting to and fro,
What time the East Wind hums his darkest hymn,
And rains beat heavy on the ruined leaf.

There, while the Autumn in the cedar trees
Sat cooped about by cloudy evergreens,
The widow sojourned on the silent road,
And mutely faced the barren mound, and plucked
A straggling shrub from thence, and passed away,
Heart-broken on to Sydney; where she took
Her passage, in an English vessel bound
To London, for her home of other years.

At rest! Not near, with Sorrow on his grave,
And roses quickened into beauty—wrapt
In all the pathos of perennial bloom;

But far from these, beneath the fretful clay
Of lands within the lone perpetual cry
Of hermit plovers and the night-like oaks,
All moaning for the peace which never comes.

At rest! And she who sits and waits behind
Is in the shadows; but her faith is sure,
And *one* fine promise of the coming days
Is breaking, like a blessed morning, far
On hills " that slope through darkness up to God."

A SPANISH LOVE SONG.

From Andalusian gardens
  I bring the rose and rue,
And leaves of subtle odour,
  To weave a gift for you.
You'll know the reason wherefore
  The sad is with the sweet!
My flowers may lie, as I would,
  A carpet for your feet.

The heart—the heart is constant!
  It holds its secret, Dear!
But often in the night time
  I keep awake for fear.
I have no hope to whisper,
  I have no prayer to send,
God save you from such passion!
  God help you from such end!

A SPANISH LOVE SONG.

You first, you last, you false love!
  In dreams your lips I kiss,
And thus I greet your Shadow,
  "Take this, and this, and this!"
When dews are on the casement,
  And winds are in the pine,
I have you close beside me—
  In sleep your mouth is mine.

I never see you elsewhere;
  You never think of me;
But fired with fever for you
  Content I am to be.
You will not turn, my Darling,
  Nor answer when I call;
But yours are soul and body
  And love of mine and all!

You splendid Spaniard! listen—
  My passion leaps to flame
For neck, and cheek, and dimple,
  And cunning shades of shame!
I tell you, I would gladly
  Give Hell myself to keep,
To cling to, half a moment,
  The lips I taste in sleep.

THE LAST OF HIS TRIBE.

He crouches, and buries his face on his knees,
    And hides in the dark of his hair;
For he cannot look up to the storm-smitten trees,
    Or think of the loneliness there:
        Of the loss and the loneliness there.

The wallaroos grope through the tufts of the grass,
    And turn to their covers for fear;
But he sits in the ashes and lets them pass
    Where the boomerangs sleep with the spear:
        With the nullah, the sling, and the spear.

Uloola, behold him! The thunder that breaks
    On the tops of the rocks with the rain,
And the wind which drives up with the salt of the lakes,
    Have made him a hunter again:
        A hunter and fisher again.

For his eyes have been full with a smouldering thought;
  But he dreams of the hunts of yore,
And of foes that he sought, and of fights that he fought
  With those who will battle no more:
    Who will go to the battle no more.

It is well that the water which tumbles and fills
  Goes moaning and moaning along;
For an echo rolls out from the sides of the hills,
  And he starts at a wonderful song:
    At the sounds of a wonderful song.

And he sees, through the rents of the scattering fogs,
  The corrobboree warlike and grim,
And the lubra who sat by the fire on the logs,
  To watch, like a mourner, for him:
    Like a mother and mourner, for him.

Will he go in his sleep from these desolate lands,
  Like a chief, to the rest of his race,
With the honey-voiced woman who beckons, and stands,
  And gleams like a Dream in his face—
    Like a marvellous Dream in his face?

ARAKOON.

Lo, in storms, the triple-headed
    Hill, whose dreaded
Bases battle with the seas,
Looms across fierce widths of fleeting
    Waters beating
Evermore on roaring leas!

Arakoon, the black, the lonely!
    Housed with only
Cloud and rain-wind, mist and damp:
Round whose foam-drenched feet, and nether
    Depths, together
Sullen sprites of thunder tramp!

ARAKOON.

There the East hums loud and surly,
    Late and early,
Through the chasms and the caves;
And across the naked verges
    Leap the surges!
White and wailing waifs of waves.

Day by day, the sea-fogs gathered—
    Tempest-fathered—
Pitch their tents on yonder peak!
Yellow drifts and fragments, lying
    Where the flying
Torrents chafe the cloven creek!

And at nightfall, when the driven
    Bolts of heaven
Smite the rock and break the bluff,
Thither troop the elves whose home is
    Where the foam is,
And the echo, and the clough.

Ever girt about with noises,
    Stormy voices,
And the salt breath of the strait,
Stands the steadfast Mountain Giant,
    Grim, reliant,
Dark as Death, and firm as Fate!

ARAKOON.

So when trouble treads, like thunder,
    Weak men under—
Treads, and breaks the thews of these—
Set thyself to bear it bravely,
    Greatly, gravely,
Like the hill in yonder seas :

Since the wrestling, and endurance
    Give assurance
To the faint at bay with pain,
That no soul to strong Endeavour
    Yoked for ever,
Works against the tide in vain.

THE VOYAGE OF TELEGONUS.

Ill fares it with the man whose lips are set
To bitter themes and words that spite the gods:
For, seeing how the son of Saturn sways
With eyes and ears for all, this one shall halt
As on hard hurtful hills; his days shall know
The plaintive front of Sorrow; level looks
With cries ill-favoured shall be dealt to him;
And *this* shall be that he may think of peace
As one might think of alienated lips
Of sweetness touched for once in kind warm dreams.
Yea, fathers of the high and holy face,
This soul thus sinning shall have cause to sob
"Ah, ah," for sleep, and space enough to learn
The wan wild Hyrie's aggregated song
That starts the dwellers in distorted heights,

With all the meaning of perpetual sighs
Heard in the mountained deserts of the world,
And where the green-haired waters glide between
The thin lank weeds and mallows of the marsh.

But thou to whom these things are like to shapes
That come of darkness—thou whose life slips past
Regarding rather these with mute fast mouth—
Hear none the less how fleet Telegonus,
The brass-clad hunter, first took oar and smote
Swift eastward-going seas, with face direct
For narrowing channels and the twofold coasts
Past Colchis and the fierce Symplegades
And utmost islands washed by streams unknown.

For in a time when Phasis whitened wide
And drove with violent waters blown of wind
Against the bare salt limits of the land,
It came to pass that, joined with Cytheræa,
The black-browed Ares, chafing for the wrong
Ulysses did him on the plains of Troy,
Set heart against the king; and when the storms
Sang high in thunder and the Thracian rain,
The god bethought him of a pale-mouthed priest
Of Thebæ, kin to ancient Chariclo,
And of an omen which the prophet gave
That touched on Death and grief to Ithaca;

Then, knowing how a heavy-handed fate
Had laid itself on Circe's brass-clad son,
He pricked the hunter with a lust that turned
All thoughts to travel and the seas remote ;
But chiefly now he stirred Telegonus
To longings for his father's exiled face,
And dreams of rest and honey-hearted love,
And quiet death with much of funeral flame
Far in the mountains of a favoured land
Beyond the wars and wailings of the waves.

So past the ridges where the coast abrupt
Dips greyly westward, Circe's strong-armed son
Swept down the foam of sharp-divided straits
And faced the stress of opening seas. Sheer out
The vessel drave ; but three long moons the gale
Moaned round ; and swift strong streams of fire revealed
The labouring rowers and the lightening surf,
Pale watchers deafened of sonorous storm,
And dripping decks and rents of ruined sails.
Yea, when the hollow ocean-driven ship
Wheeled sideways, like a chariot cloven through
In hard hot battle, and the night came up
Against strange headlands lying East and North,
Behold a black wild wind with death to all
Ran shoreward, charged with flame and thunder-smoke,

Which blew the waters into wastes of white
And broke the bark, as lightning breaks the pine;
Whereat the sea in fearful circles shewed
Unpitied faces turned from Zeus and light,
Wan swimmers wasted with their agony,
And hopeless eyes and moaning mouths of men.
But one held by the fragments of the wreck,
And Ares knew him for Telegonus,
Whom heavy-handed Fate had chained to deeds
Of dreadful note with sin beyond a name.
So, seeing this, the black-browed lord of war,
Arrayed about by Jove's authentic light,
Shot down amongst the shattered clouds and called
With mighty strain, betwixt the gaps of storm,
"Oceanus, Oceanus!" whereat
The surf sprang white, as when a keel divides
The gleaming centre of a gathered wave;
And, ringed with flakes of splendid fire of foam,
The son of Terra rose halfway and blew
The triple trumpet of the **water**-gods,
At which great winds fell back and all the sea
Grew dumb, as on the land a war-feast breaks
When deep sleep falls upon the souls of men.
Then Ares of the night-like brow made known
The brass-clad hunter of the facile feet
Hard clinging to the slippery logs of pine,
And told the omen to the hoary god
That touched on Death and grief to Ithaca;

Wherefore Oceanus with help of hand
Bore by the chin the warrior of the North,
A moaning mass, across the shallowing surge,
And cast him on the rocks of alien shores
Against a wintry morning shot with storm.

Hear also thou how mighty gods sustain
The men set out to work the ends of Fate
Which fill the world with tales of many tears,
And vex the sad face of Humanity:
Six days and nights the brass-clad chief abode
Pent up in caverns by the straightening seas,
And fed on ferns and limpets; but the dawn
Before the strong sun of the seventh, brought
A fume of fire and smells of savoury meat,
And much rejoicing, as from neighbouring feasts;
At which the hunter, seized with sudden lust,
Sprang up the crags, and, like a dream of Fear,
Leapt, shouting, at a huddled host of hinds
Amongst the fragments of their steaming food;
And, as the hoarse wood-wind in Autumn sweeps
To every zone the hissing latter leaves,
So, fleet Telegonus, by dint of spear
And strain of thunderous voice, did scatter these
East, South, and North: 'twas then the chief had rest,
Hard by the outer coast of Ithaca,
Unknown to him who ate the spoil and slept.

Nor stayed he hand thereafter; but, when noon
Burned dead on misty hills of stunted fir,
This man shook slumber from his limbs, and sped
Against hoar beaches and the kindled cliffs
Of falling waters; these he waded through,
Beholding past the forests of the West
A break of light, and homes of many men,
And shining corn, and flowers, and fruits of flowers;
Yea, seeing these, the facile-footed chief
Grasped by the knot the huge Ææan lance,
And fell upon the farmers; wherefore they
Left hoe and plough, and crouched in heights remote
Companioned with the grey-winged fogs; but he
Made waste their fields and throve upon their
  toil—
As throve the boar, the fierce four-footed curse
Which Artemis did raise in Calydon
To make stern mouths wax white with foreign fear,
All in the wild beginning of the World.

So one went down and told Laertes' son
Of what the brass-clad stranger from the straits
Had worked in Ithaca: whereat the King
Rose, like a god, and called his mighty heir,
Telemachus, the wisest of the wise;
And these two, having counsel, strode without,
And armed them with the arms of warlike days—

The helm, the javelin, and the sun-like shield,
And glancing greaves and quivering stars of steel!
Yea, stern Ulysses, rusted not with rest,
But dread as Ares, gleaming on his car
Gave out the reins; and straightway all the lands
Were struck by noise of steed and shouts of men,
And furious dust, and splendid wheels of flame.
Meanwhile the hunter (starting from a sleep
In which the pieces of a broken dream
Had shown him Circe with most tearful face),
Caught at his spear, and stood, like one at bay
When Summer brings about Arcadian horns
And headlong horses mixt with maddened hounds;
Then huge Ulysses, like a fire of fight,
Sprang sideways on the flying car, and drave
Full at the brass-clad warrior of the North
His massive spear; but fleet Telegonus
Stooped from the death, but heard the speedy lance
Sing like a thin wind through the steaming air;
Yet he, dismayed not by the dreadful foe—
Unknown to him—dealt out his strength, and aimed
A strenuous stroke at great Laertes' son,
Which missed the shield, but bit through flesh and bone,
And drank the blood, and dragged the soul from thence!
So fell the King! and one cried, "Ithaca!
Ah, Ithaca!" and turned his face and wept.

Then came another—wise Telemachus—
Who knelt beside the man of many days
And pored upon the face; but lo, the life
Was like bright water spilt in sands of thirst,
A wasted splendour swiftly drawn away.
Yet held he by the dead : he heeded not
The moaning warrior who had learnt his sin—
Who waited now, like one in lairs of pain,
Apart with darkness hungry for his fate;
For, had not wise Telemachus the lore
Which makes the pale-mouthed seer content to sleep
Amidst the desolations of the world?
So therefore he who knew Telegonus,
The child of Circe by Laertes' son,
Was set to be a scourge of Zeus, smote not
But rather sat with moody eyes, and mused,
And watched the dead. For who may brave the
    gods?

Yet, O my fathers, when the people came,
And brought the holy oils and perfect fire,
And built the pile, and sang the tales of Troy—
Of desperate travels in the olden time,
By shadowy mountains and the roaring sea,
Near windy sands and past the Thracian snows—
The man who crossed them all to see his sire,
And had a loyal heart to give the King,

Instead of blows—this man did little more
Than moan outside the fume of funeral rites,
All in a rushing twilight full of rain,
And clap his palms for sharper pains than swords.
Yea, when the night broke out against the flame,
And lonely noises loitered in the fens,
This man nor stirred nor slept, but lay at wait,
With fastened mouth. For who may brave the gods?

SITTING BY THE FIRE.

Ah! the solace in the sitting,
   Sitting by the fire,
When the wind without is calling
And the fourfold clouds are falling,
With the rain-racks intermitting,
   Over slope and spire.
Ah! the solace in the sitting,
   Sitting by the fire.

Then, and then, a man may ponder,
   Sitting by the fire,
Over fair far days, and faces
Shining in sweet-coloured places
Ere the thunder broke asunder
   Life and dear Desire.
Thus, and thus, a man may ponder,
   Sitting by the fire.

Waifs of song pursue, perplex me,
   Sitting by the fire:
Just a note, and lo, the change then!
Like a child, I turn and range then,
Till a shadow starts to vex me—
   Passion's wasted pyre.
So do songs pursue, perplex me,
   Sitting by the fire.

Night by night—the old, old story—
   Sitting by the fire,
Night by night, the dead leaves grieve me:
Ah! the touch when youth shall leave me,
Like my fathers, shrunken, hoary,
   With the years that tire.
Night by night—that old, old, story,
   Sitting by the fire.

Sing for slumber, sister Clara,
   Sitting by the fire.
I could hide my head and sleep now,
Far from those who laugh and weep now,
Like a trammelled, faint wayfarer,
   'Neath yon mountain-spire.
Sing for slumber, sister Clara,
   Sitting by the fire.

CLEONE.

Sing her a song of the sun:
   Fill it with tones of the stream,—
Echoes of waters that run
   Glad with the gladdening gleam.
Let it be sweeter than rain,
   Lit by a tropical moon:
Light in the words of the strain,
   Love in the ways of the tune.

Softer than seasons of sleep:
   Dearer than life at its best!
Give her a ballad to keep,
   Wove of the passionate West:
Give it and say of the hours—
   "Haunted and hallowed of thee,
Flower-like woman of flowers,
   What shall the end of them be?"

You that have loved her so much,
    Loved her asleep and awake,
Trembled because of her touch,
    What have you said for her sake?
Far in the falls of the day,
    Down in the meadows of myrrh,
What has she left you to say
    Filled with the beauty of her?

Take her the best of your thoughts,
    Let them be gentle and grave,
Say, "I have come to thy courts,
    Maiden, with all that I have."
So she may turn with her sweet
    Face to your love and to you,
Learning the way to repeat
    Words that are brighter than dew.

CHARLES HARPUR.

Where Harpur lies, the rainy streams,
   And wet hill-heads, and hollows weeping,
Are swift with wind, and white with gleams,
   And hoarse with sounds of storms unsleeping.

Fit grave it is for one whose song
   Was tuned by tones he caught from torrents,
And filled with mountain-breaths, and strong
   Wild notes of falling forest-currents.

So let him sleep! the rugged hymns
   And broken lights of woods above him!
And let me sing how Sorrow dims
   The eyes of those that used to love him.

As April in the wilted wold
    Turns faded eyes on splendours waning,
What time the latter leaves are old,
    And ruin strikes the strays remaining;

So we that knew this singer dead,
    Whose hands attuned the Harp Australian,
May set the face and bow the head,
    And mourn his fate and fortunes alien.

The burden of a perished faith
    Went sighing through his speech of sweetness,
With human hints of Time and Death,
    And subtle notes of incompleteness.

But when the fiery power of Youth
    Had passed away and left him nameless,
Serene as Light, and strong as Truth,
    He lived his life untired and tameless.

And, far and free, this man of men
    With wintry hair and wasted feature,
Had fellowship with gorge and glen,
    And learned the loves and runes of Nature.

Strange words of wind, and rhymes of rain,
    And whispers from the inland fountains,
Are mingled in his various strain
    With leafy breaths of piny mountains.

But, as the under-currents sigh
   Beneath the surface of a river,
The music of Humanity
   Dwells in his forest-psalms for ever.

No soul was he to sit on heights
   And live with rocks apart and scornful:
Delights of men were his delights,
   And common troubles made him mournful.

The flying forms of unknown powers
   With lofty wonder caught and filled him;
But there were days of gracious hours
   When sights and sounds familiar thrilled him.

The pathos worn by wayside things,
   The passion found in simple faces,
Struck deeper than the life of springs
   Or strength of storms and sea-swept places.

But now he sleeps, the tired bard,
   The deepest sleep; and lo, I proffer
These tender leaves of my regard
   With hands that falter as they offer.

GOD HELP OUR MEN AT SEA.

The wild night comes like an owl to its lair;
   The black clouds follow fast;
And the sun-gleams die and the lightnings glare,
   And the ships go heaving past, past, past—
   The ships go heaving past!
        Bar the doors, and higher, higher
        Pile the faggots on the fire!
        Now abroad by many a light
        Empty seats there are to-night;
        Empty seats that none may fill,
        For the storm grows louder still!
How it surges and swells through the gorges and dells,
   Under the ledges and over the lea,
Where a watery sound goeth moaning around.
        God help our men at sea!

Oh! never a tempest blew on the shore,
   But that some heart did moan
For a darling voice it would hear no more,
   And a face that had left it lone, lone, lone—
   A face that had left it lone!

I am watching by a pane
Darkened with the gusty rain;
Watching through a mist of tears,
Sad with thoughts of other years:
For a brother I did miss
In a stormy time like this.
Ah! the torrent howls past, like a fiend on the blast,
  Under the ledges and over the lea;
And the pent waters gleam, and the wild surges scream!
    God help our men at sea!

Ah, Lord, they may grope through the dark to find
  Thy hand within the gale;
And cries may rise on the wings of the wind
  From mariners weary and pale, pale, pale—
  From mariners weary and pale!
      'Tis a fearful thing to know,
      While the storm-winds loudly blow,
      That a man can sometimes come
      Too near to his father's home;
      So that he shall kneel and say,
      " Lord, I would be far away !"
Ho! the hurricanes roar round a dangerous shore,
  Under the ledges and over the lea;
And there twinkles a light on the billows so white—
    God help our men at sea!

COOGEE.

Sing the song of wave-worn Coogee—Coogee in the
    distance white
With its jags and points disrupted, gaps and fractures
    fringed with light!
Haunt of gledes and restless plovers of the melan-
    choly wail
Ever lending deeper pathos to the melancholy gale.
There, my brothers, down the fissures, chasms deep
    and wan and wild,
Grows the sea-bloom, one that blushes like a shrink-
    ing fair blind child;
And amongst the oozing forelands many a glad green
    rock-vine runs,
Getting ease on earthy ledges sheltered from Decem-
    ber suns.

Often, when a gusty morning, rising cold and gray
    and strange,
Lifts its face from watery spaces, vistas full with
    cloudy change;

Bearing up a gloomy burden which anon begins to
    wane,
Fading in the sudden shadow of a dark determined
    rain;
Do I seek an eastern window, so to watch the
    breakers beat
Round the steadfast crags of Coogee, dim with drifts
    of driving sleet:
Hearing hollow mournful noises sweeping down a
    solemn shore
While the grim sea-caves are tideless and the storm
    strives at their core.

Often when the floating vapours fill the silent autumn
    leas,
Dreamy memories fall like moonlight over silver
    sleeping seas,
Youth and I and Love together!—other times and
    other themes
Come to me unsung, unwept for, through the faded
    evening gleams:
Come to me and touch me mutely—I that looked
    and longed so well,
Shall I look and yet forget them? who may know or
    who foretell?
Though the southern wind roams, shadowed with its
    immemorial grief,

Where the frosty wings of Winter leave their white-
    ness on the leaf?

Friend of mine beyond the waters, here and here
    these perished days
Haunt me with their sweet dead faces and their old
    divided ways.
You that helped and you that loved me, take this
    song and when you read
Let the lost things come about you, set your
    thoughts and hear and heed:
Time has laid his burden on us: we who wear our
    manhood now—
We would be the boys we *have* been, free of heart
    and bright of brow—
Be the boys for just an hour, with the splendour
    and the speech
Of thy lights and thunders, Coogee, flying up thy
    gleaming beach!

Heart's desire and heart's division! who would come
    and say to me
With the eyes of far-off friendship, "You are as
    you used to be"?
Something glad and good has left me here with
    sickening discontent,
Tired of looking, neither knowing, what it was or
    where it went.

So it is this sight of Coogee, shining in the morning dew,
Sets me stumbling through dim summers once on fire with youth and you.
Summers pale as southern evenings when the year has lost its power,
And the wasted face of April weeps above the withered flower.

Not that seasons bring no solace—not that time lacks light and rest;
But the old things were the dearest, and the old loves seem the best.
We that start at songs familiar—we that tremble at a tone,
Floating down the ways of music, like a sigh of sweetness flown,
We can never feel the freshness—never find again the mood
Left amongst fair-featured places brightened of our brotherhood;
This, and this, we have to think of, when the night is over all,
And the woods begin to perish, and the rains begin to fall.

OGYGES.

Stand out, swift-footed leaders of the horns,
And draw strong breath, and fill the hollowy cliff
With shocks of clamour,—let the chasm take
The noise of many trumpets, lest the hunt
Should die across the dim Aonian hills,
Nor break through thunder and the surf-white cave
That hems about the old-eyed Ogyges
And bars the sea-wind, rain-wind, and the sea!

Much fierce delight hath old-eyed Ogyges
[A hairless shadow in a lion's skin]
In tumult, and the gleam of flying spears,
And wild beasts vexed to death; "for," sayeth he,
" Here lying broken, do I count the days
For very trouble; being like the tree—
The many-wintered father of the trunks

On yonder ridges: wherefore it is well
To feel the dead blood kindling in my veins
At sound of boar or battle; yea to find
A sudden stir, like life, about my feet,
And tingling pulses through this frame of mine
What time the cold clear dayspring, like a bird
Afar off, settles on the frost-bound peaks,
And all the deep blue gorges, darkening down,
Are filled with men and dogs and furious dust!"

So in the time whereof thou weetest well—
The melancholy morning of the World—
He mopes or mumbles, sleeps or shouts for glee,
And shakes his sides—a cavern-hutted King!
But when the ouzel in the gaps at eve
Doth pipe her dreary ditty to the surge
All tumbling in the soft green level light,
He sits as quiet as a thick-mossed rock,
And dreameth in his cold old savage way
Of gliding barges on the wine-dark waves,
And glowing shapes, and sweeter things than sleep,
But chiefly, while the restless twofold bat
Goes flapping round the rainy caves above,
Where one broad opening letteth in the moon,
He starteth, thinking of that gray-haired man,
His sire: then oftentimes the white-armed child
Of thunder-bearing Jove, young Thebe, comes
And droops above him with her short sweet sighs

For Love distraught—for dear Love's faded sake
That weeps and sings and weeps itself to death
Because of casual eyes, and lips of frost,
And careless mutterings, and most weary years.

Bethink you, doth the wan Ægyptian count
This passion, wasting like an unfed flame,
Of any worth now; seeing that his thighs
Are shrunken to a span; and that the blood
Which used to spin tumultuous down his sides
Of life in leaping moments of desire,
Is drying like a thin and sluggish stream
In withered channels—think you, doth he pause
For golden Thebe and her red young mouth?

Ah, golden Thebe—Thebe, weeping there,
Like some sweet wood-nymph wailing for a rock,
If Octis with the Apollonian face—
That fair-haired prophet of the sun and stars—
Could take a mist and dip it in the West
To clothe thy limbs of shine about with shine
And all the wonder of the amethyst,
He'd do it—kneeling like a slave for thee!
If he could find a dream to comfort thee,
He'd bring it: thinking little of his lore,
But marvelling greatly at those eyes of thine.
Yea, if the Shepherd waiting for thy steps,
Pent down amongst the dank black-weeded rims,

Could shed his life like rain about thy feet,
He'd count it sweetness past all sweets of love
To die by thee—his life's end in thy sight.

O but he loves the hunt, doth Ogyges!
And therefore should we blow the horn for him:
He, sitting mumbling in his surf-white cave
With helpless feet and alienated eyes,
Should hear the noises nathless dawn by dawn
Which send him wandering swiftly through the days
When like a springing cataract he leapt
From crag to crag, the strongest in the chase
To spear the lion, leopard, or the boar!
O but he loves the hunt; and, while the shouts
Of mighty winds are in this mountained World,
Behold the white bleak woodman, Winter, halts
And bends to him across a beard of snow
For wonder; seeing Summer in his looks
Because of dogs and calls from throats of hair
All in the savage hills of Hyria!
And, through the yellow evenings of the year,
What time September shows her mooned front
And poppies burnt to blackness droop for drouth,
The dear Demeter, splashed from heel to thigh
With spinning vine-blood, often stoops to him
To crush the grape against his wrinkled lips
Which sets him dreaming of the thickening wolves
In darkness, and the sound of moaning seas.

So with the blustering tempest doth he find
A stormy fellowship : for when the North
Comes reeling downwards with a breath like spears,
Where Dryope the lonely sits all night
And holds her sorrow crushed betwixt her palms,
He thinketh mostly of that time of times
When Zeus the Thunderer—broadly-blazing King—
Like some wild comet beautiful but fierce,
Leapt out of cloud and fire and smote the tops
Of black Ogygia with his red right hand,
At which great fragments tumbled to the Deeps—
The mighty fragments of a mountain-land—
And all the World became an awful Sea !

But, being tired, the hairless Ogyges
Best loveth night and dim forgetfulness !
" For," sayeth he, " to look for sleep is good
When every sleep is as a sleep of death
To men who live, yet know not why they live,
Nor how they live ! I have no thought to tell
The people when this time of mine began ;
But forest after forest grows and falls,
And rock by rock is wasted with the rime,
While I sit on and wait the end of all ;
Here taking every footstep for a sign ;
An ancient shadow whiter than the foam !"

BY THE SEA.

The caves of the sea have been troubled to-day
   With the water which whitens, and widens, and
      fills;
And a boat with our brother was driven away
   By a wind that came down from the tops of the hills.
Behold I have seen on the threshold again
   A face in a dazzle of hair!
Do you know that she watches the rain, and the main,
   And the waves which are moaning there?
     Ah, moaning and moaning there!

Now turn from your casements, and fasten your doors,
   And cover your faces, and pray, if you can;
There are wails in the wind, there are sighs on the
      shores,
   And alas, for the fate of a storm-beaten man!
Oh, dark falls the night on the rain-rutted verge,
   So sad with the sound of the foam!
Oh, wild is the sweep and the swirl of the surge;
   And his boat may never come home!
     Ah, never and never come home!

SONG OF THE CATTLE-HUNTERS.

While the morning light beams on the fern-matted
    streams,
  And the water-pools flash in its glow,
Down the ridges we fly, with a loud ringing cry—
  Down the ridges and gullies we go!
And the cattle we hunt, they are racing in front,
  With a roar like the thunder of waves;
As the beat and the beat of our swift horses' feet
  Start the echoes away from their caves!
      As the beat and the beat
      Of our swift horses' feet
    Start the echoes away from their caves!

Like a wintery shore that the waters ride o'er,
  All the lowlands are filling with sound;
For swiftly we gain where the herds on the plain,
  Like a tempest, are tearing the ground!

And we'll follow them hard to the rails of the yard,
   Over gulches and mountain-tops grey,
Where the beat and the beat of our swift horses'
     feet
   Will die with the echoes away!
        Where the beat and the beat
     Of our swift horses' feet
   Will die with the echoes away!

KING SAUL AT GILBOA.

With noise of battle and the dust of fray,
Half-hid in fog, the gloomy mountain lay;
But Succoth's watchers from their outer fields
Saw fits of flame and gleams of clashing shields
For where the yellow river draws its spring
The hosts of Israel travelled thundering!
There, beating like the storm that sweeps to sea
Across the reefs of chafing Galilee,
The car of Abner and the sword of Saul
Drave Gaza down Gilboa's southern wall;
But swift and sure the spears of Ekron flew,
Till peak and slope were drenched with bloody dew!
"Shout, Timnath, shout!" the blazing leaders cried,
And hurled the stone, and dashed the stave aside:
"Shout, Timnath, shout! Let Hazor hold the height,
Bend the long bow and break the lords of fight!"
From every hand the swarthy strangers sprang,
Chief leaped on chief, with buckler buckler rang!
The flower of armies! set in Syrian heat,
The ridges clamoured under labouring feet;

Nor stayed the warriors till from Salim's road
The crescent horns of Abner's squadrons glowed.
Then, like a shooting splendour on the wing,
The strong-armed son of Kish came thundering;
And as in Autumn's fall, when woods are bare,
Two adverse tempests meet in middle air,
So Saul and Achish; grim with heat and hate,
Met by the brooks and shook the scales of Fate;
For now the struggle swayed, and, firm as rocks
Against the storm-wind of the equinox,
The rallied lords of Judah stood and bore
All day the fiery tides of fourfold war.

But he that fasted in the secret cave,
And called up Samuel from the quiet grave,
And stood with darkness and the mantled ghosts
A bitter night on shrill Samarian coasts,
Knew well the end: of how the futile sword
Of Israel would be broken by the Lord;
How Gath would triumph with the tawny line
That bend the knee at Dagon's brittle shrine;
And how the race of Kish would fall to wreck
Because of vengeance stayed at Amalek;
Yet strove the sunlike king, nor rested hand
Till yellow evening filled the level land;
Then Judah reeled before a biting hail
Of sudden arrows shot from Akor's vale,

Where Libnah, lapped in blood from thigh to heel,
Drew the tense string and pierced the quivering steel.
There fell the sons of Saul, and, man by man,
The chiefs of Israel up to Jonathan;
And, while swift Achish stooped and caught the spoil,
Ten chosen archers red with sanguine toil
Sped after Saul, who, faint and sick and sore
With many wounds, had left the thick of war:
He, like a baffled bull by hunters prest,
Turned sharp about and faced the flooded west,
And saw the star-like spears and moony spokes
Gleam from the rocks and lighten through the oaks;
A sea of splendour! How the chariots rolled
On wheels of blinding brightness manifold!
While stumbling over spike and spine and spur
Of sultry lands, escaped the son of Ner
With smitten men! At this the front of Saul
Grew darker than a blasted tower wall;
And seeing how there crouched upon his right
Aghast with fear a black Amalekite,
He called and said, "I pray thee, man of pain,
Red from the scourge, and recent from the chair,
Set thou thy face to mine and stoutly stand
With yonder bloody sword-hilt in thine hand
And fall upon me." But the faltering hind
Stood trembling like a willow in the wind.
Then further, Saul: "Lest Ashdod's vaunting hosts
Should bear me captive to their bleak-blown coasts,

I pray thee, smite me : seeing peace has fled,
And rest lies wholly with the quiet dead."
At this a flood of sunset broke, and smote
Keen blazing sapphires round a kingly throat,
Touched arm and shoulder, glittered in the crest,
And made swift starlights on a jewelled breast!
So, starting forward like a loosened hound,
The stranger clutched the sword and wheeled it
    round,
And struck the Lord's Anointed! Fierce and fleet,
Philistia came with shouts and clattering feet;
By gaping gorges and by rough defile,
Dark Ashdod beat across a dusty mile;
Hot Hazor's bowmen toiled from spire to spire;
And Gath sprang upwards like a gust of fire!
On either side did Libnah's lords appear;
And brass-clad Timnath thundered in the rear!
"Mark, Achish, mark!"—South-west and south there
    sped
A dabbled hireling from the dreadful dead!
"Mark, Achish, mark!"—The mighty front of Saul,
Great in his life and god-like in his fall!
This was the arm that broke Philistia's pride
Where Kishon chafes his seaward-going tide!
This was the sword that smote till set of sun
Red Gath from Michmash unto Ajalon!
Low in the dust. And Israel scattered far!
And dead the trumps, and crushed the hoofs of war!

So fell the king! as it was said by him
Who hid his forehead in a mantle dim
At bleak Endor, what time unholy rites
Vext the long sleep of still Samarian heights:
For bowed to earth before the hoary Priest
Did he of Kish withstand the smoking feast,
To fast, in darkness and in sackcloth rolled,
And house with wild things in the biting cold;
Because of sharpness lent to Gaza's sword,
And Judah widowed by the angry Lord.

So Silence came! As when the outer verge
Of Carmel takes the white and whistling surge,
Hoarse hollow noises fill the caves and roar
Along the margins of the echoing shore,
Thus War had thundered! But as Evening breaks
Across the silver of Assyrian lakes,
When reapers rest, and through the level red
Of sunset, peace like holy oil is shed,
Thus Silence fell; but Israel's daughters crept
Outside their thresholds, waited, watched, and wept.

Then they that dwell beyond the flats and fens
Of sullen Jordan, and in gelid glens
Of Jabesh-Gilead, chosen chiefs and few,
Around their loins the hasty girdle drew,
And faced the forests huddled fold on fold,
And dells of glimmering greenness manifold,

What time Orion in the west did set
A shining foot on hills of wind and wet:
These journeyed nightly till they reached the capes
Where Ashdod revelled over heated grapes;
And, while the feast was loud and scouts were turned,
From Saul's bound body cord by cord they burned,
And bore the king athwart the place of tombs,
And hasted eastward through the tufted glooms;
Nor broke the cake, nor stayed the step till Morn
Shot over Debir's cones and crags forlorn!

From Jabesh then the weeping virgins came;
In Jabesh then they built the funeral flame;
With costly woods they piled the lordly pyre,
Brought yellow oils and fed the perfect fire;
While round the crescent stately Elders spread
The flashing armour of the mighty dead,
With crown and spear, and all the trophies won
From many wars by Israel's dreadful Son.
Thence, when the feet of Evening paused and stood
On shadowy mountains and the roaring flood
(As through a rushing twilight full of rain
The weak Moon looked athwart Gadara's plain),
The younger warriors bore the urn, and broke
The humid turf about a wintering oak,
And buried Saul; and, fasting, went their ways,
And hid their faces seven nights and days.

IN THE VALLEY.

Said the yellow-haired Spirit of Spring
   To the white-footed Spirit of Snow,
"On the wings of the tempest take wing,
   And leave me the valleys, and go."
And, straightway, the streams were unchained,
   And the frost-fettered torrents broke free,
And the strength of the winter-wind waned
   In the dawn of a light on the sea.

Then a morning-breeze followed and fell,
   And the woods were alive and astir
With the pulse of a song in the dell,
   And a whisper of day in the fir.
Swift rings of sweet water were rolled
   Down the ways where the lily-leaves grew,
And the green, and the white, and the gold,
   Were wedded with purple and blue.

But the lips of the flower of the rose
    Said, "where is the ending hereof?
Is it sweet with you, life, at the close?
    Is it sad to be emptied of love?"
And the voice of the flower of the peach
    Was tender and touching in tone,
"When each has been grafted on each,
    It is sorrow to live on alone."

Then the leaves of the flower of the vine
    Said, "what will there be in the day
When the reapers are red with my wine,
    And the forests are yellow and grey?"
And the tremulous flower of the quince
    Made answer, "three seasons ago
My sisters were star-like, but since,
    Their graves have been made in the snow."

Then the whispering flower of the fern
    Said, "who will be sad at the death,
When Summer blows over the burn,
    With the fierceness of fire in her breath?"
And the mouth of the flower of the sedge
    Was opened to murmur and sigh,
"Sweet wind-breaths that pause at the edge
    Of the nightfall, and falter, and die."

TWELVE SONNETS.

I.

A MOUNTAIN SPRING.

Peace hath an altar there. The sounding feet
   Of thunder, and the 'wildering wings of rain,
Against fire-rifted summits flash and beat,
   And through grey upper gorges swoop and strain;
   But round that hallowed mountain-spring remain,
Year after year, the days of tender heat,
And gracious nights whose lips with flowers are sweet,
   And filtered lights, and lutes of soft refrain.
A still bright pool. To men I may not tell
   The secret that its heart of water knows—
   The story of a loved and lost repose;
Yet *this* I say to cliff, and close-leaved dell:
A fitful Spirit haunts yon limpid well,
   Whose likeness is the faithless face of Rose.

II.

LAURA.

If Laura—lady of the flower-soft face—
   Should light upon these verses, she may take
The tenderest line, and through its pulses trace
   What man can suffer for a woman's sake.
   For in the nights that burn, the days that break,
A thin pale Figure stands in Passion's place;
And Peace comes not, nor yet the perished grace
   Of Youth to keep old faiths and fires awake.
Ah, marvellous maid! Life sobs, and sighing saith,
   " She left me, fleeting like a fluttered dove;
But I would have a moment of her breath,
   So I might taste the sweetest sense thereof,
   And catch from blossoming, honeyed lips of love
Some faint, some fair, some dim delicious death."

III.

BY A RIVER.

But red ripe mouth and brown luxurious eyes
   Of her I love, by all your sweetness shed
In far fair days, on one whose memory flies
   To faithless lights and gracious speech gainsaid,
   I pray you, when yon river-path I tread,
Make with the woodlands some soft compromise
Lest they should vex me into fruitless sighs
   With visions of a woman's gleaming head!
For every green and golden-hearted thing
   That gathers beauty in that shining place
Beloved of beams and wooed by wind and wing,
   Is rife with glimpses of her marvellous face;
And in the whispers of the lips of Spring
   The music of her lute-like voice I trace.

IV.

ATTILA.

WHAT though his feet were shod with sharp fierce
    flame,
  And Death and Ruin were his daily squires,
The Scythian helped by Heaven's thunders came:
  The time was ripe for God's avenging fires.
  Lo, loose lewd trulls and lean luxurious liars
Had brought the fair fine face of Rome to shame
And made her one with sins beyond a name—
  That queenly daughter of imperial sires!
The blood of elders like the blood of sheep
  Was dashed across the circus! Once, while din,
And dust, and lightnings, and a daggled heap
Of beast-slain men made lords with laughter leap,
  Night fell, with rain. The Earth so sick of sin
Had turned her face into the dark to weep.

V.

A REWARD.

BECAUSE a steadfast flame of clear intent
    Gave force and beauty to full-actioned life;
Because his way was one of firm ascent,
    Whose stepping-stones were hewn of change and strife;
Because as husband loveth noble wife,
He loved fair Truth; because the thing he meant
To do, that thing he did, nor paused, nor bent,
    In face of poor and pale conclusions; yea,
Because of this, how fares the Leader dead?
    What kind of mourners weep for him to-day?
What golden shroud is at his funeral spread?
    Upon his brow what leaves of laurel, say?
    About his breast is tied a sackcloth grey,
And knots of thorns deface his lordly head.

VI.

TO ———

A HANDMAID to the Genius of thy Song
   Is sweet fair Scholarship. 'Tis she supplies
   The fiery Spirit of the passioned eyes
With subtle syllables whose notes belong
   To some chief source of perfect melodies.
And, glancing through a laurelled lordly throng
   Of shining singers, lo, my vision flies
To William Shakespeare! he it is whose strong
   Full flute-like music haunts thy stately Verse.
A worthy Levite of his court thou art!
   One sent amongst us to defeat the curse
That binds us to the Actual. Yea, thy part,
O lute-voiced lover, is to lull the heart
   Of love repelled: its darkness to disperse.

VII.

THE STANZA OF CHILDE HAROLD.

Who framed the stanza of Childe Harold? He
   It was who, halting on a stormy shore,
   Knew well the lofty Voice which evermore
In grand distress doth haunt the sleepless sea
   With solemn sounds! And as each wave did roll
   Till one came up, the mightiest of the whole,
To sweep and surge across a vacant lea,
Wild words were wedded to wild melody!
   This Poet must have had a speechless sense
   Of some dead Summer's boundless affluence!
Else, whither can we trace the passioned lore
Of Beauty, steeping to the very core
   His royal Verse? And that rare light which lies
   About it like a Sunset in the skies?

VIII.

A LIVING POET.

HE knows the sweet vexation in the strife
   Of Love with Time, this Bard who fain would stray
To fairer place beyond the storms of Life,
   With astral faces near him day by day.
In deep-mossed dells the mellow waters flow
Which best he loves; for there the echoes, rife
With rich suggestions of his Long Ago,
   Astarte! pass with thee. And, far away,
Dear Southern Seasons haunt the dreamy eye :
Spring, flower-zoned, and Summer, warbling low
In tasselled corn, alternate come and go;
While gipsy Autumn, splashed from heel to thigh
With vine-blood, treads the leaves; and, halting nigh,
Wild Winter bends across a beard of snow.

IX.

DANTE AND VIRGIL.

When lost Francesca sobbed her broken tale
  Of Love, and Sin, and boundless Agony;
While that wan Spirit by her side did wail
  And bite his lips for utter misery—
  The Grief which could not speak, nor hear, nor see;
So tender grew the superhuman face
Of one who listened, that a mighty trace
  Of superhuman Woe gave way, and pale,
The sudden light upstruggled to its place;
  While all his limbs began to faint and fail
With such excess of Pity! But, behind,
  The Roman Virgil stood—the calm, the wise—
  With not a shadow in his regal eyes,
A stately type of all his stately kind!

x.

REST.

Sometimes we feel so spent for want of rest,
  We have no thought beyond. I know to-day,
  When tired of bitter lips and dull delay
With faithless words, I cast mine eyes upon
The shadows of a distant mountain-crest,
And said, "That hill must hide within its breast
Some secret glen secluded from the sun.
  O, mother Nature! would that I could run
Outside to thee, and, like a wearied guest
  Half blind with lamps and sick of feasting, lay
An aching head on thee. Then down the streams
  The moon might swim; and I should feel her
    grace,
While soft winds blew the sorrows from my face
So quiet in the fellowship of dreams."

XI.

AFTER PARTING.

I CANNOT tell what change hath come to you
    To vex your splendid hair. I only know
One Grief: the Passion left betwixt us two,
    Like some forsaken watchfire, burneth low.
'Tis sad to turn and find it dying so
Without a hope of resurrection! Yet,
    O radiant face that found me tired and lone,
I shall not for the dear·dead Past forget
    The sweetest looks of all the Summers gone.
Ah! Time hath made familiar wild Regret;
    For now the leaves are white in last year's bowers;
And now doth sob along the ruined leas
The homeless storm from saddened southern seas,
    While March sits weeping over withered flowers.

XII.

ALFRED TENNYSON.

The silvery dimness of a happy dream
   I've known of late. • Methought where Byron
      moans,
   Like some wild gulf in melancholy zones,
I passed tear-blinded! Once a lurid gleam
   Of stormy sunset loitered on the sea
While, travelling troubled, like a straitened stream,
   The voice of Shelley died away from me!
   Still sore at heart I reached a lake-lit lea;
And then, the green-mossed glades with many a
      grove
Where lies the calm which Wordsworth used to love;
   And lastly, Locksley Hall! from whence did rise
A haunting Song that blew, and breathed, and blew,
With rare delights: 'twas *there* I woke and knew
   The sumptuous comfort left in drowsy eyes.

SUTHERLAND'S GRAVE.

[*The first white man buried in Australia.*]

ALL night long the sea out yonder—all night long the wailful sea,
Vext of winds and many thunders, seeketh rest unceasingly!
Seeketh rest in dens of tempest where, like one distraught with pain,
Shouts the wild-eyed sprite, Confusion: seeketh rest, and moans in vain!
Ah, but you should hear it calling, calling when the haggard sky
Takes the darks and damps of Winter with the mournful marsh-fowls' cry;
Even while the strong, swift torrents from the rainy ridges come
Leaping down and breaking backwards—million coloured shapes of foam!

Then, and then, the sea out yonder chiefly looketh
    for the boon
Portioned to the pleasant valleys, and the grave sweet
    summer moon:
Boon of Peace, the still, the saintly, spirit of the
    dewdells deep—
Yellow dells, and hollows haunted by the soft dim
    dreams of sleep.

All night long the flying water breaks upon the
    stubborn rocks—
Ooze-filled forelands burnt and blackened, smit and
    scarred with lightning shocks;
But above the tender sea-thrift—but beyond the
    flowering fern,
Runs a little pathway westward—pathway quaint
    with turn on turn—
Westward trending, thus it leads to shelving shores
    and slopes of mist:
Sleeping shores, and glassy bays of green and gold
    and amethyst!
There tread gently—*gently*, pilgrim; *there* with
    thoughtful eyes look round;
Cross thy breast and bless the silence: lo, the place
    is holy ground!
Holy ground for ever, stranger! All the quiet silver
    lights

Dropping from the starry heavens through the soft
    Australian nights—
Dropping on those lone grave-grasses—come serene,
    unbroken, clear,
Like the love of God the Father, falling, falling, year
    by year!
Yea, and like a Voice supernal, *there* the daily wind
    doth blow
In the leaves above the Sailor buried ninety years
    ago.

SYRINX.

A HEAP of low dark rocky coast
   Unknown to foot or feather!
A sea-voice moaning like a ghost;
   And fits of fiery weather!

The flying Syrinx turned and sped
   By dim mysterious hollows,
Where night is black, and day is red,
   And frost the fire-wind follows!

Strong heavy footfalls in the wake,
   Came up with flights of water:
The gods were mournful for the sake
   Of Ladon's lovely daughter.

For when she came to spike and spine,
   Where reef and river gather,
Her feet were sore with shell and chine;
   She could not travel farther.

Across a naked strait of land,
   Blown sleet and surge were humming;
But trammelled with the shifting sand,
   She heard the monster coming!

A thing of hoofs, and horns, and lust!
   A gaunt goat-footed stranger!
She bowed her body in the dust,
   And called on Zeus to change her.

And called on Hermes fair and fleet,
   And her of hounds and quiver,
To hide her in the thickets sweet
   That sighed above the river.

So He that sits on flaming wheels,
   And rules the sea and thunder,
Caught up the satyr by the heels,
   And tore his skirts in sunder.

While Arcas of the glittering plumes
  Took Ladon's daughter lightly,
And set her in the gracious glooms
  That mix with moon-mist nightly.

And touched her lips with wild-flower wine;
  And changed her body slowly,
Till in soft reeds of song and shine
  Her life was hidden wholly.

ON THE PAROO.

As when the strong stream of a wintering sea
Rolls round our coast, with bodeful breaks of storm,
And swift salt rain, and bitter wind that saith
Wild things and woeful of the White South Land
Alone with God and Silence in the cold—
As when this cometh, men from dripping doors
Look forth, and shudder for the mariners
Abroad, so we for absent brothers looked
In days of drought, and when the flying floods
Swept boundless: roaring down the bald, black, plains
Beyond the farthest spur of western hills.

For where the Barwân cuts a rotten land,
Or lies unshaken, like a great blind creek,
Between hot mouldering banks, it came to this,
All in a time of short and thirsty sighs,
That thirty rainless months had left the pools
And grass as dry as ashes: then it was
Our kinsman started for the lone Paroo,

From point to point, with patient strivings, sheer
Across the horrors of the windless downs,
Blue-gleaming like a sea of molten steel.

But never drought had broke them: never flood
Had quenched them: they with mighty youth and
    health,
And thews and sinews knotted like the trees—
They, like the children of the native woods,
Could stem the strenuous waters, or outlive
The crimson days and dull dead nights of thirst
Like camels! yet of what avail was strength
Alone to them—though it was like the rocks
On stormy mountains—in the bloody time
When fierce sleep caught them in the camps at rest,
And violent darkness gripped the life in them
And whelmed them, as an eagle unawares
Is whelmed and slaughtered in a sudden snare.

All murdered by the blacks! smit while they lay
In silver dreams, and with the far faint fall
Of many waters breaking on their sleep!
Yea, in the tracts unknown of any man
Save savages—the dim-discovered ways
Of footless silence or unhappy winds—
The wild men came upon them, like a fire
Of desert thunder; and the fine firm lips

That touched a mother's lips a year before,
And hands that knew a dearer hand than life,
Were hewn like sacrifice before the stars,
And left with hooting owls, and blowing clouds,
And falling leaves, and solitary wings!

Ay, you may see their graves—you who have toiled,
And tripped, and thirsted, like these men of ours;
For verily I say that *not* so deep
Their bones are that the scattered drift and dust
Of gusty days will never leave them bare.
O dear, dead, bleaching bones! I know of those
Who have the wild strong will to go and sit
Outside all things with you, and keep the ways
Aloof from bats, and snakes, and trampling feet
That smite your peace and theirs—who have the heart
Without the lusty limbs to face the fire,
And moonless midnights, and to be indeed,
For very sorrow, like a moaning wind
In wint'ry forests with perpetual rain.

Because of this—because of sisters left
With desperate purpose and dishevelled hair,
And broken breath, and sweetness quenched in tears—
Because of swifter silver for the head,
And furrows for the face—because of these
That should have come with Age, that come with Pain,

O Master! Father! sitting where our eyes
Are tired of looking, say for once are we—
Are *we* to set our lips with weary smiles
Before the bitterness of Life and Death,
And call it honey, while we bear away
A taste like wormwood?

        Turn thyself, and sing—
Sing, Son of Sorrow! Is there any gain
For breaking of the loins, for melting eyes,
And knees as weak as water? any peace,
Or hope, for casual breath, and labouring lips,
For clapping of the palms, and sharper sighs
Than frost; or any light to come for those
Who stand and mumble in the alien streets
With heads as grey as Winter? any balm
For pleading women, and the love that knows
Of nothing left to love?

        They sleep a sleep
Unknown of dreams, these darling friends of ours.
And *we* who taste the core of many tales
Of tribulation—*we* whose lives are salt
With tears indeed—we therefore hide our eyes
And weep in secret lest our grief should risk
The rest that hath no hurt from daily racks
Of fiery clouds and immemorial rains.

FAITH IN GOD.

Have faith in God. For whosoever lists
   To calm conviction in these days of strife,
Will learn that in this steadfast stand exists
   The scholarship severe of human life—

This face to face with Doubt! I know how strong
   His thews must be who fights, and falls, and bears,
By sleepless nights, and vigils lone and long,
   And many a woeful wraith of wrestling prayers;

Yet trust in Him! not in an old Man throned
   With thunders on an everlasting cloud,
But in that awful Entity, enzoned
   By no wild wraths nor bitter homage loud.

When from the summits of some sudden steep
   Of Speculation, you have strength to turn
To things too boundless for the broken sweep
   Of finite comprehension, wait and learn

That God hath been "His own interpreter"
  From first to last;—so you will understand
The tribe who best succeed when men most err
  To suck through fogs the fatness of the land.

One thing is surer than the autumn tints
  We saw last week in yonder river bend,
That all our poor expression helps and hints,
  However vaguely, to the solemn end

That God is Truth. And if our dim ideal
  Fall short of fact—so short that we must weep,
Why shape specific sorrows, though the real
  Be not the song which erewhile made us sleep?

Remember, Truth draws upward! This, to us,
  Of steady happiness should be a cause
Beyond the differential calculus,
  Or Kant's dull dogmas and mechanic laws.

A man is manliest when he wisely knows
  How vain it is to halt, and pule, and pine,
Whilst under every mystery haply flows
  The finest issue of a love divine.

MOUNTAIN MOSS.

It lies amongst the sleeping stones,
   Far down the hidden mountain-glade;
And past its brink the torrent moans
   For ever in a dreamy shade:

A little patch of dark-green moss,
   Whose softness grew of quiet ways,
(With all its deep, delicious floss,)
   In slumb'rous suns of summer days.

You know the place? With pleasant tints
   The broken sunset lights the bowers;
And then the woods are full with hints
   Of distant, dear, voluptuous flowers!

'Tis often now the pilgrim turns
   A faded face towards that seat,
And cools his brow amongst the ferns:
   The runnel dabbling at his feet.

There fierce December seldom goes,
   With scorching step, and dust, and drouth;
But, soft and low, October blows
   Sweet odours from her dewy mouth.

And Autumn, like a gipsy bold,
   Doth gather near it grapes and grain,
Ere Winter comes, the woodman old,
   To lop the leaves in wind and rain.

O, greenest moss of mountain glen,
   The face of Rose is known to thee;
But we shall never share with men
   A knowledge dear to Love and me!

For are they not between us saved,
   The words my darling used to say;
What time the western waters laved
   The forehead of the fainting Day!

Cool comfort had we on your breast
    While yet the fervid Noon burned mute
O'er barley field and barren crest,
    And leagues of gardens flushed with fruit.

Oh! sweet and low, we whispered so;
    And sucked the pulp of plum and peach:
But it was many years ago,
    When each, you know, was loved of each.

THE GLEN OF ARRAWATTA.

A SKY of wind! And while these fitful gusts
Are beating round the windows in the cold,
With sullen sobs of rain, behold I shape
A Settler's story of the wild old times:
One told by camp-fires when the station-drays
Were housed and hidden, forty years ago;
While swarthy drivers smoked their pipes, and drew,
And crowded round the friendly-gleaming flame
That lured the dingo howling from his caves
And brought sharp sudden feet about the brakes.

A tale of Love and Death. And shall I say
A tale of Love *in* Death; for all the patient eyes
That gathered darkness, watching for a son
And brother, never dreaming of the fate—
The fearful fate he met alone, unknown,
Within the ruthless Australasian wastes?

For, in a far-off sultry Summer rimmed
With thunder-cloud and red with forest-fires,
All day, by ways uncouth and ledges rude,
The wild men held upon a stranger's trail
Which ran against the rivers and athwart
The gorges of the deep blue western hills.

And when a cloudy sunset, like the flame
In windy evenings on the Plains of Thirst
Beyond the dead banks of the far Barcoo,
Lay heavy down the topmost peaks, they came
With pent-in breath and stealthy steps, and crouched,
Like snakes, amongst the grasses, till the Night
Had covered face from face and thrown the gloom
Of many shadows on the front of things.

There, in the shelter of a nameless glen
Fenced round by cedars and the tangled growths
Of blackwood stained with brown and shot with grey,
The jaded white-man built his fire, and turned
His horse adrift amongst the water-pools
That trickled underneath the yellow leaves
And made a pleasant murmur, like the brooks
Of England through the sweet autumnal noons.

Then after he had slaked his thirst, and used
The forest-fare, for which a healthful day
Of mountain-life had brought a zest, he took

His axe, and shaped with boughs and wattle-forks
A wurley, fashioned like a bushman's roof:
The door brought out athwart the strenuous flame:
The back thatched in against a rising wind.

And, while the sturdy hatchet filled the clifts
With sounds unknown, the immemorial haunts
Of echoes sent their lonely dwellers forth
Who lived a life of wonder: flying round
And round the glen—what time the kangaroo
Leapt from his lair and huddled with the bats—
Far-scattering down the wildly-startled fells.
Then came the doleful owl; and evermore
The bleak morass gave out the bittern's call;
The plover's cry; and many a fitful wail
Of chilly omen, falling on the ear
Like those cold flaws of wind that come and go
An hour before the break of day.

       Anon
The stranger held from toil, and, settling down,
He drew rough solace from his well-filled pipe
And smoked into the night: revolving there
The primal questions of a squatter's life;
For in the flats, a short day's journey past
His present camp, his station yards were kept
With many a lodge and paddock jutting forth

Across the heart of unnamed prairie-lands,
Now loud with bleating and the cattle bells
And misty with the hut-fire's daily smoke.

Wide spreading flats, and western spurs of hills
That dipped to plains of dim perpetual blue;
Bold summits set against the thunder-heaps;
And slopes be-hacked and crushed by battling kine!
Where now the furious tumult of their feet
Gives back the dust and up from glen and brake
Evokes fierce clamour, and becomes indeed
A token of the squatter's daring life,
Which growing inland—growing year by year,
Doth set us thinking in these latter days,
And makes one ponder of the lonely lands
Beyond the lonely tracks of Burke and Wills,
Where, when the wandering Stuart fixed his camps
In central wastes afar from any home
Or haunt of man, and in the changeless midst
Of sullen deserts and the footless miles
Of sultry silence, all the ways about
Grew strangely vocal and a marvellous noise
Became the wonder of the waxing glooms.

Now, after Darkness, like a mighty spell
Amongst the hills and dim dispeopled dells,
Had brought a stillness to the soul of things,
It came to pass that, from the secret depths

Of dripping gorges, many a runnel-voice
Came, mellowed with the silence, and remained
About the caves, a sweet though alien sound:
Now rising ever, like a fervent flute
In moony evenings, when the theme is love:
Now falling, as ye hear the Sunday bells
While hastening fieldward from the gleaming town.

Then fell a softer mood; and Memory paused
With faithful Love, amidst the sainted shrines
Of Youth and Passion in the valleys past
Of dear delights which never grow again.
And if the stranger (who had left behind
Far anxious homesteads in a wave-swept isle
To face a fierce sea-circle day by day,
And hear at night the dark Atlantic's moan)
Now took a hope and planned a swift return,
With wealth and health and with a youth unspent,
To those sweet ones that stayed with Want at home,
Say *who* shall blame him—though the years are long,
And Life is hard, and waiting makes the heart grow
    old?

Thus passed the time until the Moon serene
Stood over high dominion like a dream
Of Peace: within the white-transfigured woods;
And o'er the vast dew-dripping wilderness
Of slopes illumined with her silent fires.

Then far beyond the home of pale red leaves
And silver sluices, and the shining stems
Of runnel-blooms, the dreamy wanderer saw,
The wilder for the vision of the Moon,
Stark desolations and a waste of plain
All smit by flame and broken with the storms:
Black ghosts of trees, and sapless trunks that stood
Harsh hollow channels of the fiery noise
Which ran from bole to bole a year before,
And grew with ruin, and was like, indeed,
The roar of mighty winds with wintering streams
That foam about the limits of the land,
And mix their swiftness with the flying seas.

Now, when the man had turned his face about
To take his rest, behold the gem-like eyes
Of ambushed wild things stared from bole and brake
With dumb amaze and faint-recurring glance,
And fear anon that drove them down the brush;
While from his den the dingo, like a scout
In sheltered ways, crept out and cowered near
To sniff the tokens of the stranger's feast
And marvel at the shadows of the flame.

Thereafter grew the wind; and chafing depths
In distant waters sent a troubled cry
Across the slumb'rous Forest; and the chill
Of coming rain was on the sleeper's brow,

When, flat as reptiles hutted in the scrub,
A deadly crescent crawled to where he lay—
A band of fierce fantastic savages
That, starting naked round the faded fire,
With sudden spears and swift terrific yells,
Came bounding wildly at the white man's head,
And faced him, staring like a dream of Hell!

Here let me pass! I would not stay to tell
Of hopeless struggles under crushing blows;
Of how the surging fiends with thickening strokes
Howled round the Stranger till they drained his strength;
How Love and Life stood face to face with Hate
And Death; and then how Death was left alone
With Night and Silence in the sobbing rains.

So, after many moons, the searchers found
The body mouldering in the mouldering dell
Amidst the fungi and the bleaching leaves,
And buried it; and raised a stony mound
Which took the mosses: then the place became
The haunt of fearful legends, and the lair
Of bats and adders.

There he lies and sleeps
From year to year: in soft Australian nights;
And through the furnaced noons; and in the times

Of wind and wet ! yet never mourner comes
To drop upon that grave the Christian's tear
Or pluck the foul dank weeds of death away.

But while the English Autumn filled her lap
With faded gold, and while the reapers cooled
Their flame-red faces in the clover grass,
They looked for him at home ; and when the frost
Had made a silence in the morning lanes,
And cooped the farmers by December fires,
They looked for him at home: and through the days
Which brought about the million-coloured Spring
With moon-like splendours in the garden plots,
They looked for him at home : while Summer danced,
A shining singer, through the tasselled corn,
They looked for him at home. From sun to sun
They waited. Season after season went,
And Memory wept upon the lonely moors,
And Hope grew voiceless, and the watchers passed,
Like shadows, one by one, away.

                        And he,
Whose fate was hidden under forest leaves,
And in the darkness of untrodden dells,
Became a marvel. Often by the hearths
In winter nights, and when the wind was wild
Outside the casements, children heard the tale

Of how he left their native vales behind
(Where he had been a child himself) to shape
New fortunes for his father's fallen house;
Of how he struggled—how his name became,
By fine devotion and unselfish zeal,
A name of beauty in a selfish land;
And then, of how the aching hours went by,
With patient listeners praying for the step
Which never crossed the floor again. So passed
The tale to children; but the bitter end
Remained a wonder, like the unknown grave
Alone with God and Silence in the hills.

EUTERPE.

Child of Light, the bright, the birdlike! wilt thou
    float and float to me
Facing winds, and sleets, and waters, flying glimpses
    of the sea?
Down amongst the hills of tempest where the elves
    of tumult roam—
Blown wet shadows of the summits, dim sonorous
    sprites of foam?
Here, and here, my days are wasted, shorn of leaf,
    and stript of fruit:
Vexed because of speech half-spoken, Maiden with
    the marvellous lute!
Vexed because of songs half-shapen, smit with fire,
    and mixed with pain:

Part of thee, and part of Sorrow, like a sunset pale
    with rain.
Child of Light, the bright, the bird-like! wilt thou
    float and float to me
Facing winds, and sleets, and waters, flying glimpses
    of the sea?

All night long, in fluent pauses, falling far, but full,
    but fine,
Faultless friend of flowers and fountains, do I hear
    that voice of thine.
All night long, amidst the burden of the lordly storm,
    that sings
High above the tumbled forelands, fleet and fierce
    with thunderings!
Then, and then, my love, Euterpe, lips of life replete
    with dreams
Murmur for thy sweet sharp fragments dying down
    Lethean streams:
Murmur for thy mouth's marred music, splendid
    hints that burn and break
Heavy with excess of beauty: murmur for thy music's
    sake.
All night long in fluent pauses, falling far, but full,
    but fine,
Faultless friend of flowers and fountains, do I hear
    that voice of thine.

In the yellow flame of evening, sound of thee doth
    come and go
Through the noises of the river and the drifting of
    the snow:
In the yellow flame of evening—at the setting of the
    day—
Sound that lightens, falls, and lightens, flickers, faints,
    and fades away.
I am famished of thy silence—broken for the tender
    note
Caught with its surpassing passion—caught and
    strangled in thy throat!
We have nought to help thy trouble—nought for
    that which lieth mute
On the harpstring and the lutestring and the spirit
    of the lute.
In the yellow flame of evening sound of thee doth
    come and go
Through the noises of the river and the drifting of
    the snow.

Daughter of the dead red summers! men that laugh
    and men that weep,
Call thee Music—shall I follow, choose their name,
    and turn, and sleep?
What thou art, behold, I know not; but thy honey
    slakes and slays

Half the want which whitens manhood in the stress
　　of alien days!
Even as a wondrous woman struck with love and
　　great desire
Hast thou been to me, Euterpe! half of tears and
　　half of fire.
But thy joy is swift and fitful; and a subtle sense of
　　pain
Sighs through thy melodious breathing, takes the
　　rapture from thy strain.
Daughter of the dead red summers! men that laugh
　　and men that weep,
Call thee Music—shall I follow, choose their name
　　and turn, and sleep?

ELLEN RAY.

A QUIET song for Ellen—
   The patient Ellen Ray,
A dreamer in the nightfall,
   A watcher in the day.
The wedded of the sailor
   Who keeps so far away:
A shadow on his forehead
   For patient Ellen Ray.

When autumn winds were driving
   Across the chafing bay,
He said the words of anger
   That wasted Ellen Ray:
He said the words of anger
   And went his bitter way:
Her dower was the darkness—
   The patient Ellen Ray.

Your comfort is a phantom,
    My patient Ellen Ray;
You house it in the night-time
    It fronts you in the day;
And when the moon is very low
    And when the lights are grey,
You sit and hug a sorry hope,
    My patient Ellen Ray!

You sit and hug a sorry hope—
    Yet who will dare to say,
The sweetness of October
    Is not for Ellen Ray?
The bearer of a burden
    Must rest at fall of day;
And you have borne a heavy one,
    My patient Ellen Ray.

AT DUSK.

At dusk, like flowers that shun the day,
   Shy thoughts from dim recesses break,
And plead for words I dare not say
    For your sweet sake.

My early love! my first, my last!
   Mistakes have been that both must rue,
But all the passion of the past
    Survives for you.

The tender message Hope might send,
   Sinks fainting at the lips of speech;
For, are you lover—are you friend,
    That I would reach?

How much to-night I'd give to win
    A banished peace—an old repose!
But here I sit, and sigh, and sin
    When no one knows.

The stern, the steadfast reticence
    Which made the dearest phrases halt,
And checked a first and finest sense,
    Was not my fault.

I held my words because there grew
    About my life persistent pride;
And you were loved who never knew
    What love could hide.

This purpose filled my soul like flame
    To win you wealth, and take the place
Where care is not, or any shame
    To vex your face.

I said, "till then my heart must keep
    Its secret safe and unconfest;"
And days and nights unknown to sleep
    The vow attest.

Yet, O my Sweet, it seems so long
   Since you were near, and fates retard
The sequel of a struggle strong,
     And Life is hard!

Too hard when one is left alone
   To wrestle Passion, never free
To turn and say to you, " My own,
     Come home to me."

SAFI.

Strong pinions bore Safi, the Dreamer,
　　Through the dazzle and whirl of a race ;
And the Earth, raying up in confusion,
　　Like a sea thundered under his face !

And the Earth raying up in confusion
　　Passed flying and flying afar,
Till it dropped like a moon into silence,
　　And waned from a moon to a star.

Was it light—was it shadow he followed
　　That he swept through those desperate tracts
With his hair beating back on his shoulders
　　Like the tops of the wind-hackled flax ?

"I come," murmured Safi the Dreamer,
 "I come, but thou fliest before!
But thy way hath the breath of the honey,
 And the scent of the myrrh evermore."

His eyes were the eyes of a watcher
 Held on by luxurious faith,
And his lips were the lips of a longer
 Amazed with the beauty of Death.

"For ever and ever," he murmured,
 "My love for the sweetness with thee,
Do I follow thy footsteps," said Safi,
 "Like the wind on a measureless sea."

And, fronting the furthermost spaces,
 He kept through the distances dim,
Till the days, and the years, and the cycles,
 Were lost and forgotten by him.

·
———

When he came to the silver star-portals,
 The Queen of that wonderful place
Looked forth from her towers resplendent,
 And started, and dreamed in his face.

And one said, "this is Safi the Only,
    Who lived in a planet below,
And housed him apart from his fellows,
    A million of ages ago.

"He erred, if he suffers, to clutch at
    High lights from the wood and the street;
Not caring to see how his brothers
    Were content with the things at their feet."

But she whispered "Ah, turn to the Stranger!
    He looks like a lord of the land;
For his eyes are the eyes of an angel,
    And the thought on his forehead is grand!

"Is there never a peace for the sinner
    Whose sin is in this that he mars
The light of his worship of Beauty,
    Forgetting the flower for the stars?"

"Behold him, my Sister immortal,
    And doubt that he knoweth his shame,
Who raves in the shadow for sweetness,
    And gloats on the ghost of a flame!

"His sin is his sin, if he suffers,
   Who wilfully straitened the Truth ;
And his doom is his doom, if he follows
   A lie without sorrow or ruth."

———

And another from uttermost verges
   Ran out with a terrible voice—
"Let him go—it is well that he goeth
   Though he break with the lot of his choice."

———

"I come," murmured Safi the Dreamer,
   "I come, but thou fliest before !
But thy way hath the breath of the honey,
   And the scent of the myrrh evermore."

———

"My Queen," said the first of the Voices,
   "He hunteth a perilous wraith,
Arrayed with voluptuous fancies
   And ringed with tyrannical faith.

"Wound up in the heart of his error
   He must sweep through the silences dire,
Like one in the dark of a desert
   Allured by fallacious fire."

And she faltered, and asked, like a doubter,
   "When he hangs on those Spaces sublime
With the Terror that knoweth no limit,
   And holdeth no record of Time,—

"Forgotten of God and the demons—
   Will he keep to his fancy amain?
Can he live for that horrible Chaos
   Of flame and perpetual rain?"

But an answer as soft as a prayer
   Fell down from a high hidden Land,
And the words were the words of a language
   Which none but the gods understand.

IN MEMORIAM.

DANIEL HENRY DENIEHY.

TAKE the harp, but very softly for our brother touch
    the strings :
Wind and wood shall help to wail him, waves and
    mournful mountain-springs.
Take the harp, but very softly, for the friend who
    grew so old
Through the hours we would not hear of—nights we
    would not fain behold!
Other voices, sweeter voices, shall lament him year
    by year,
Though the morning finds us lonely, though we sit
    and marvel here:
Marvel much while Summer cometh trammelled with
    November wheat,

Gold about her forehead gleaming, green and gold
    about her feet;
Yea, and while the land is dark with plover, gull,
    and gloomy glede,
Where the cold swift songs of Winter fill the inter-
    lucent reed.

Yet my harp, and O, my fathers, never look for
    Sorrow's lay,
Making life a mighty darkness in the patient noon
    of day;
Since he resteth whom we loved so, out beyond
    these fleeting seas,
Blowing clouds, and restless regions paved with old
    perplexities,
In a land where thunder breaks not, in a place
    unknown of snow,
Where the rain is mute for ever, where the wild
    winds never go:
Home of far-forgotten phantoms—genii of our
    peaceful prime,
Shining by perpetual waters past the ways of Change
    and Time:
Haven of the harried spirit, where it folds its
    wearied wings,
Turns its face and sleeps a sleep with deep forget-
    fulness of things.

His should be a grave by mountains, in a cool and
    thick-mossed lea,
With the lone creek falling past it—falling ever to
    the sea.
His should be a grave by waters, by a bright and
    broad lagoon,
Making steadfast splendours hallowed of the quiet-
    shining moon.
There the elves of many forests—wandering winds
    and flying lights—
Born of green, of happy mornings, dear to yellow
    summer nights,
Full of dole for him that loved them, then might
    halt, and then might go,
Finding fathers of the people to their children
    speaking low—
Speaking low of one who, failing, suffered all the
    poet's pain,
Dying with the dead leaves round him—hopes which
    never grow again.

MEROPE.

Far in the ways of the hyaline wastes—in the face
    of the splendid
Six of the sisters—the star-dowered sisters ineffably
    bright,
Merope sitteth, the shadow-like wife of a monarch
    unfriended
Of Ades—of Orcus, the fierce, the implacable god
    of the night.
Merope—fugitive Merope! lost to thyself and thy
    lover,
Cast, like a dream, out of thought, with the moons
    which have passed into sleep,
What shall avail thee? Alcyone's tears, or the
    sight to discover
Of Sisyphus pallid for thee by the blue, bitter, lights
    of the deep?

Pallid, but patient for sorrow? O, thou of the fire
    and the water,
Half with the flame of the sunset and kin to the
    streams of the sea,
Hast thou the songs of old times for desire of thy
    dark-featured daughter,
Sweet with the lips of thy yearning, O Æthra:
    with tokens of thee?
Songs that would lull her, like kisses forgotten of
    silence where speech was
Less than the silence that bound it as Passion is
    bound by a ban;
Seeing we know of thee, Mother, *we* turning and
    hearing how each was
Wrapt in the other ere Merope faltered and fell for
    a man?
Mortal she clave to, forgetting her birthright,
    forgetting the lordlike
Sons of the Many-winged Father, and chiefs of the
    plume and the star,
Therefore, because that her sin was the grief of the
    grand and the godlike,
Sitteth thy child than a morning-moon bleaker, the
    faded, and far.
Ringed with the flowerlike Six of the Seven, arrayed
    and anointed
Ever with beautiful pity, she watches, she weeps, and
    she wanes,

Blind as a flame on the hills of the Winter in hours appointed
For the life of the foam and the thunder—the strength of the imminent rains.
Who hath a portion, Alcyone, like her? Asterope, fairer
Than sunset on snow, and beloved of all brightness, say what is there left
Sadder and paler then Pleione's daughter disconsolate bearer
Of trouble that smites like a sword of the gods to the break of the heft?
Demeter, and Dryope, known to the forests, the falls, and the fountains,
Yearly, because of their walking, and wailing, and wringing of hands,
Are they as one with this woman? or Hyrie wild in the mountains,
Breaking her heart in the frosts and the fires of the uttermost lands?
These have their bitterness. This, for Persephone, that, for Œchalian
Homes, and the lights of a kindness blown out with the stress of her shame:
One for her child, and one for her sin; but thou above all art an alien,
Girt with the halos that vex thee, and wrapt in a grief beyond name.

Yet sayeth Sisyphus—Sisyphus, stricken and chained
    of the Minioned
Kings of great darkness, and trodden in dust by the
    feet of the fates,
" Sweet are the ways of thy watching, and pallid and
    perished and pinioned,
Moon amongst maidens, I leap for thy love like a
    god at the gates—
Leap for the dreams of a rose of the heavens, and
    beat at the portals
Paved with the pain of unsatisfied pleadings for thee
    and for thine,
But Zeus is immutable Master, and these are the
    walls the Immortals
Build for our sighing, and who may set lips at the
    lords and repine?
Therefore," he saith, " I am sick for thee, Merope,
    faint for the tender
Touch of thy mouth, and the eyes like the lights of
    an altar to me;
But lo, thou art far, and thy face is a still and
    a sorrowful splendour!
And the storm is abroad with the rain on the perilous
    straits of the sea."

AFTER THE HUNT.

Underneath the windy mountain walls
   Forth we rode, an eager band,
By the surges, and the verges, and the gorges,
   Till the night was on the land—
   On the hazy, mazy land!
Far away the bounding prey
   Leapt across the ruts and logs,
But we galloped, galloped, galloped on,
   Till we heard the yapping of the dogs!
   The yapping and the yelping of the dogs.

Oh! it was a madly merry day
   We shall not so soon forget,
And the edges, and the ledges, and the ridges,
   Haunt us with their echoes yet—
   Echoes, echoes, echoes yet!
While the moon is on the hill
   Gleaming through the streaming fogs,
Don't you gallop, gallop, gallop still?
   Don't you hear the yapping of the dogs—
The yapping and the yelping of the dogs?

ROSE LORRAINE.

Sweet water-moons, blown into lights
   Of flying gold on pool and creek,
And many sounds, and many sights,
   Of younger days, are back this week.
I cannot say I sought to face,
   Or greatly cared to cross again,
The subtle spirit of the place
   Whose life is mixed with Rose Lorraine.

What though her voice rings clearly through
   A nightly dream I gladly keep,
No wish have I to start anew
   Heart-fountains that have ceased to leap.
Here, face to face with different days,
   And later things that plead for love,
It would be worse than wrong to raise
   A phantom far too fain to move.

But, Rose Lorraine—ah, Rose Lorraine,
   I'll whisper now where no one hears.
If you should chance to meet again
   The man you kissed in soft dead years,
Just say for once " he suffered much,"
   And add to this " his fate was worst
Because of me, my voice, my touch,"—
   There is no passion like the first!

If I that breathe your slow sweet name
   As one breathes low notes on a flute,
Have vext your peace with word of blame,
   The phrase is dead—the lips are mute.
Yet when I turn towards the wall,
   In stormy nights, in times of rain,
I often wish you could recall
   Your tender speeches, Rose Lorraine.

Because, you see, I thought them true,
   And did not count you self-deceived,
And gave myself in all to you,
   And looked on Love as Life achieved.
Then came the bitter, sudden change,
   The fastened lips, the dumb despair:
The first few weeks were very strange,
   And long, and sad, and hard to bear.

No woman lives with power to burst
    My passion's bonds, and set me free;
For Rose is last where Rose was first,
    And only Rose is fair to me.
The faintest memory of her face,
    The wilful face that hurt me so,
Is followed by a fiery trace
    That Rose Lorraine must never know.

I keep a faded ribbon string
    You used to wear about your throat;
And of this pale, this perished thing,
    I think I know the threads by rote.
God help such love! To touch your hand,
    To loiter where your feet might fall,
You marvellous girl, my soul would stand
    The worst of hell—its fires and all!

THE END.

www.ingramcontent.com/pod-product-compliance
Lightning Source LLC
Chambersburg PA
CBHW030244170426
43202CB00009B/621